Voice Your Opinion

Atsushi Iino   Sayo Nakamura   Brian Wistner

Toshihiko Wada   Yukiko Yabuta

KINSEIDO

Kinseido Publishing Co., Ltd.

3-21 Kanda Jimbo-cho, Chiyoda-ku,
Tokyo 101-0051, Japan

First published 2023 by Kinseido Publishing Co., Ltd.

Design   DAITECH co., ltd.
Illustrations Hiroaki Katsube
Photo   p. 52 © David Tonelson | Dreamstime.com

 音声ファイル無料ダウンロード

https://www.kinsei-do.co.jp/download/4179

この教科書で 🎧 DL 00 の表示がある箇所の音声は、上記 URL または QR コードにて
無料でダウンロードできます。自習用音声としてご活用ください。

▶ PC からのダウンロードをお勧めします。スマートフォンなどでダウンロードされる場合は、
 ダウンロード前に「解凍アプリ」をインストールしてください。
▶ URL は、**検索ボックスではなくアドレスバー (URL 表示欄) に入力**してください。
▶ お使いのネットワーク環境によっては、ダウンロードできない場合があります。

🔘 CD 00　左記の表示がある箇所の音声は、教室用 CD（Class Audio CD）に収録されています。

はしがき

　本書は「英語が話せるようになる」ことを目的とした教科書です。英語が「話せるようになる」ためには主に4つの課題があります。その課題を克服するため、本書では「話すこと」を軸にした4技能の総合的な育成を目指しました。

　課題の1つ目は話す内容となる知識・情報です。本書の英文は、賛否両論または二者択一の時事的な問題を取り上げて、知識を整理してインプットできるようにしました。リスニングとリーディングの両方、また、ディベートにも活用できる素材です。また、硬い話題ばかりでなく、若者が身近に感じる話題と身近でなくても教養を高められるメッセージ性の高い題材を、硬軟織り交ぜて配置しました。

　2つ目は知識に基づいた思考力です。本書では思考力を養うための対話活動を各章に2回配置しました。1回目は、ペアになって自らの考えに根拠を交えながら自由に話すInteractionの活動、2回目は、話題に関する意見の論点を客観的かつ論理的に組み立てて話す力を育むRole Play Discussionの活動です。前者は話者の主体的な選択による自己表現のやりとりです。後者は自らの意見とは関係なくロールプレイの役割に応じて論点を客観的に把握し、意思決定者役を説得するために論拠を工夫して話す活動です。このように、2つの異なる観点から思考力を高め、発信力を伸ばすことを目指します。

　3つ目の課題は話すための言語能力です。本書はFormulaic Expressionsを中心に構成されています。Formulaic Expressionsは高校までの文法シラバスでは扱いが薄い語用論的な知識ですが、これらの表現を場面に応じて学び、使いこなすことで自分の意見を相手に明確に伝えることができます。また、Focus on Formとしてリスニング用対話文の理解後に置いた音読とシャドーイングの中で発音への注意を促しました。さらに、本文の内容理解後に語彙・文法についても扱いました。

　4つ目の課題は話した英語を話しっぱなしにせず、振り返ることです。本書では、InteractionやRole Play Discussionの後に自らのスピーキングを振り返る機会、そしてWrite Your OpinionにおいてはRole Play Discussionで話した内容をパラグラフ・ライティングでまとめる活動を用意し、次の発信につなげられるよう工夫しました。

　以上のように、本書は、話すために聞く、話すために読む、話した内容を書くといった「話すこと」を軸として技能統合を図りながら「アウトプット・インターアクションを目途としたインプット重視の英語教育」を目指します。従来の「学んで覚えてから使う」（知識先行型）から「使うために学ぶ・使って間違えながら学ぶ」（運用先行型）という、英語教育のパラダイム・シフトに応える教材です。

　尚、本書を刊行するにあたり、金星堂の四條雪菜様、戸田浩平様、蔦原美智様には多くの助言と補助を頂きました。この場をお借りして感謝の意を表します。

著者一同

本書の構成とねらい

Listen and **Interact**	*1st Round*	対話内容のスキャニング：短い会話を聞いて、1人の意見または質問について他の4人が表明している意見を判断します。細部は聞き取れなくてもよいので、キーとなる部分に注意しましょう。
	2nd Round A	*Formulaic Expressions* の確認：囲みの中の表現の意味を理解して、発音を確認しましょう。
	2nd Round B	スキャニング：*1st Round* の会話をもう一度聞いて、囲みの中のどの表現が使われているか確認しましょう。
	3rd Round	2回聞いた会話を、今度は文字を見ながら聞いて、空欄に入る語句を書き取りましょう。文字と音声を結びつけながら、意味を確認しましょう。
	Focus on Sounds	音読と発音：*1st Round* の会話の内容や表現を確認しながら自分のペースで音読をしましょう。また、「発音ポイント」にも注意を払って声に出してみましょう。 パラレル音読：文字と音声のつながりを緊密にするため、英文を見ながらモデル音声を聞いた直後に声に出してみましょう。また、意味にも注意が向くようにしましょう。 シャドーイング：モデル音声を聞こえたそばから再現するように声に出し、自分のことばとして表現のレパートリーを増やしましょう。
	Idea Generation	討論するための意見づくり：2つの異なる視点からの意見を読み、どちらの視点に基づく考えかを判断しましょう。話題に関する情報を整理して自分の知識として取り込みましょう。
	Interaction	友達との自由対話：話題に関してクラスメイトと意見交換をしましょう。自分の意見に根拠や具体例を添えて対話をなるべく長く続けましょう。その中で*Formulaic Expressions*を意識して使ってみましょう。
Gather Information	*Listening*	概要理解のためのリスニング：話題に関するプレゼンテーションを聞きながら、事実や2つの異なる意見のキーワードをノートとしてメモしましょう。
	Reading	読解：ノートを取るために聞いたプレゼンテーションの英文を、今度は文字で読んで内容を確認しましょう。

	Focus on Meaning	再読：問題文が本文の内容と合致するかしないかを判断しましょう。答えを探すために再度英文を読み直すなどして理解を深め、発信するための知識にしましょう。	
	Focus on Vocabulary	語彙学習：英文で使われている語の同義語または反意語を判断する課題を通して、語の意味を確認しましょう。文脈から意味を推測したり、選択肢の語の意味も確認したりして語彙を増やしましょう。	
	Focus on Grammar	文法学習：英文で使われている文法を理解し、確認しましょう。**Role Play Discussion**で自分が英語を使うときに意識して使ってみましょう。	
Role Play Discussion	*Situation*	場面・役割と対話：3人一組のグループを組んで役割ごとに相手への質問や説得方法を考えて英語で話しましょう。メモをキーワードレベルで準備し、右側の**Cue Expressions**を活用しながら話し合いましょう。*Formulaic Expressions*や、これまで学習した論点や表現を積極的に使い、考えながら話しましょう。	
	Decision Making	結果発表：意思決定者役は、客観的に説得力のある意見に基づいて最終的な決断を下し、その結果と理由を他の2人に説明しましょう。また、クラスで結果を共有しましょう。	
	Review Your Role Play	対話の振り返り：論理的な話し方、*Formulaic Expressions*や学んだ文法項目がどのくらい使えたかなどを振り返りましょう。	
Write Your Opinion	ライティング：*Theme*に従って、**Role Play Discussion**の意思決定者役になった場合の意見をパラグラフ・ライティングの形式で書きましょう。これまでに学んだ内容や語句・表現を積極的に使いましょう。 Review Your Writing（自己チェック）：書いた作文をチェック項目に応じて自分で確認し、必要に応じて書き直しましょう。		
Further Activities	調べ学習と発表：*Example*を参考に、海外の事情やテーマに関する詳細な情報をグループなどで調べて発表し合いましょう。		

はしがき
本書の構成とねらい

Table of Contents

Unit 1

Which is better for a holiday, camping or staying at a hotel?

旅といえば
キャンプ派？ ホテル派？

近年、旅行の傾向としてキャンプが人気
になってきています。旅行中の宿泊形態
はキャンプが良いか、ホテルが良いか考
えてみましょう。

Listen *and* Interact

1st Round

Ray の意見に対する友達の意見を聞き、表にチェックを入れましょう。

Ray's opinion: I prefer staying at a hotel.

 DL 02　CD1-02

	Emma	Yota	Sophia	Tim
Prefers camping	☐	☐	☐	☐
Prefers staying at a hotel	☐	☐	☐	☐

2nd Round

A. 次の表現の意味を確認し、音声に続いて声に出してみましょう。

B. 再度 *1st Round* の音声を聞き、使われている次の表現に○をつけましょう。

 DL 03　CD1-03

Formulaic Expressions　　*Introducing Points of View*

🔵 順序立てて話すとき

First of all, ...　　To begin with, ...　　First, ... Second, ... Third, ...
Lastly, ...　　Finally, ...

🔵 情報を追加するとき

Also, ...　　Furthermore, ...　　In addition, ...　　Moreover, ...
As for ..., ...　　Speaking of ..., ...　　Regarding ..., ...

Ray: I'm planning to visit a national park next summer with a friend. He said he wants to try camping, but I personally want to stay at a hotel. What do you think, Emma?

Emma: ¹_____, why do you want to stay at a hotel in a national park? Camping is a lot of fun. For example, you can listen to the birds singing and watch the ²_____ from your tent! What do you think, Yota?

Yota: I totally agree with you, Emma. You can have a wonderful time ³_____ _____. In addition, camping is less ⁴_____ than staying at a hotel. You don't need to pay for a room, and you can reduce the ⁵_____ for your meals.

Ray: I see. What do you think, Sophia?

Sophia: I think there could be hygiene problems when camping. Usually, water ⁶_____ is difficult. You sometimes can't take a ⁷_____ for several days. I prefer staying in a clean hotel room. Which do you prefer, Tim?

Tim: ⁸_____, I prefer staying at a hotel. You can access the Internet all the time in a hotel. However, it is difficult to get a stable ⁹_____ when you stay at a ¹⁰_____ campground.

Focus on Sounds

1st Roundの音声を利用して、音読とシャドーイングを行いましょう。内容を理解しながら発音ポイントにも注意し、表に沿って5点満点で自己評価しましょう。

発音ポイント ▶ 音の連結　But_I personally want to stay at_a hotel. [ℓ.2]

音読 テキストを見ながら音読		内容・発音を意識して読めた度合い				
		5	4	3	2	1
パラレル音読 テキストを見ながら音声と同時に音読		内容・発音を意識して言えた度合い				
		5	4	3	2	1
シャドーイング テキストを見ないで音声の直後に復唱		ついていけた度合い				
		5	4	3	2	1

Idea Generation

1～5の文を読み、キャンプ派(a)かホテル派(b)かを判断しましょう。

1. You can sleep in a comfortable bed. **a | b**
2. Hotel accommodations are too expensive. **a | b**
3. You have access to clean water all the time. **a | b**
4. You can easily explore lakes and mountains. **a | b**
5. Camping allows you to cook anything you like. **a | b**

Interaction

これまでの内容を参考にして、下線部に語句を補いながら対話をしましょう。

A: Which is better for a holiday, camping or staying at a hotel?

B: I think _____ is better for a holiday.

A: Can you tell me more about your opinion?

B: **First of all,** _____. **In addition,** ...

⤵ うまく言えなかった内容を英語でどう表現するか調べ、クラスメイトと共有しましょう。

Gather Information

Listening

プレゼンテーションの音声を聞いてキーワードを書き取りましょう。

🎧 DL 04　◉ CD1-04 ～ ◉ CD1-08

Facts

Advantages of camping	Advantages of staying at a hotel

次の英文を読んで、内容を理解しましょう。後の設問にも答えましょう。

DL 04   CD1-04 ~ CD1-08

Which is better for a holiday, camping or staying at a hotel?

1 Traveling is a popular way to spend holidays. Some people prefer staying at a hotel to relax in a well-equipped room and enjoy warm hospitality from the staff. Others want to camp in a park and experience the outdoors.

2 According to a survey in 2019, more than eight million people in Japan went camping by automobile. Even during the coronavirus pandemic, camping maintained its popularity. In 2020, the ratio of beginner campers was about one fourth, which means many people started camping for fun. On the other hand, a survey conducted by a travel agency showed that more than 40% of the respondents preferred to stay in a clean hotel. They also preferred having meals inside their rooms. These facts indicate that more people are trying different ways to enjoy their holidays.

3 Now, let's look at the advantages of camping. First, camping usually costs less than staying at a hotel. When camping, you need to pay only for your camping space regardless of the number of guests. Second, camping is an excellent way to wash your everyday stress away. You can enjoy all that nature offers such as fresh air in the woods and clear water in the river. It is scientifically proven that spending time in nature lowers the level of chemicals in the brain that cause stress. Third, you can spend your holiday with your pets. Few hotels allow pets to stay with you. However, many campsites are pet-friendly.

4 How about staying in a hotel? First, you don't need to worry about hygiene when you stay in a hotel. Fresh towels and linens are provided, and rooms are cleaned almost

every day. Furthermore, you can feel safer in a hotel. Your room can be locked. To prevent anything dangerous from happening, some hotels have security cameras and even security guards. Lastly, you can receive a variety of services. Hotel staff are usually kind and polite to the guests. Nice hotels often offer something special such as bottles of water and snacks.

30   5   To conclude, the right choice depends on your traveling needs. If you like outdoor activities, camping may be the way. If you need clean and secure accommodations, a hotel might be the best option.

(367 words)

Focus on Meaning

本文の内容と一致するものはT、一致しないものはFを選びましょう。

1. The number of campers in Japan has been decreasing.   T | F
2. About 25% of campers went camping for the first time in 2020.   T | F
3. Staying close to nature is an advantage of camping.   T | F
4. Many hotels are pet-friendly these days.   T | F
5. Some campgrounds have security guards.   T | F

Focus on Vocabulary

本文に登場する1〜5の語の同義語 ⊟ または反意語 ⟺ として最も適切な語を選びましょう。

1. well-equipped   [ℓ.2]   ⊟ well-furnished   well-balanced   well-known   well-designed
2. hospitality   [ℓ.2]   ⟺ welcome   warmth   sickness   unfriendliness
3. maintain   [ℓ.5]   ⊟ brush   keep   damage   obtain
4. hygiene   [ℓ.19]   ⟺ a [clean   sanitary   healthy   dirty] condition
5. accommodation   [ℓ.31]   ⊟ a place to [visit   talk   stay   question]

Focus on Grammar   名詞句

名詞に修飾語句をつけて説明するときは、〈形容詞＋名詞〉のように修飾語句が名詞の前にくる形のほかに、修飾語句が後ろにくる場合もあります（something / nothingの後の形容詞や関係代名詞による後置修飾など）。

例   **warm hospitality** / Tourists can find **something local** for souvenirs.
    形容詞＋名詞   名詞＋形容詞

You can enjoy all **that nature offers**.
        └── 関係代名詞による修飾節

Task   第4段落の〈名詞＋形容詞〉の名詞句に下線を引き、意味を確認しましょう。

Role Play Discussion

Situation を読み、3人一組となっ
てそれぞれの役割に分かれディス
カッションをしましょう。メモは
キーワードレベルで準備し、右ペー
ジの表現例も参考にしながら、細
部は考えながら話しましょう。

Situation

クラブ仲間が夏休み中の旅行計画をして
います。クラブ長はキャンプにするかホテ
ル泊にするか迷っています。部員Aはキャンプを、
部員Bはホテルをすすめています。部員の意見を
聞き、クラブ長はどちらの宿泊形態にするか決定
しましょう。

 Memo

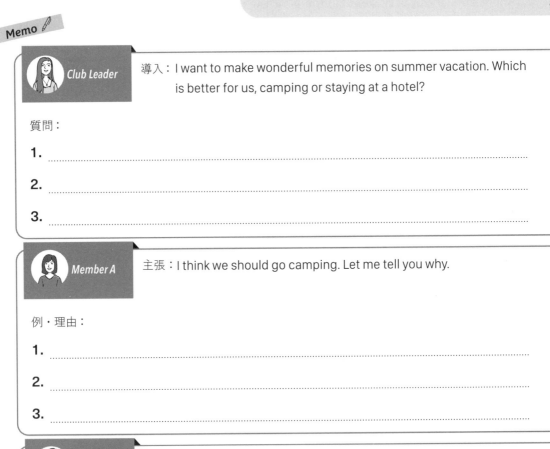

Club Leader

導入：I want to make wonderful memories on summer vacation. Which is better for us, camping or staying at a hotel?

質問：

1. ....

2. ....

3. ....

Member A

主張：I think we should go camping. Let me tell you why.

例・理由：

1. ....

2. ....

3. ....

Member B

主張：I think we should stay at a hotel. I'll tell you why.

例・理由：

1. ....

2. ....

3. ....

- What we have to decide is ...
- What is good about camping / staying at a hotel?
- Have you ever gone camping with your friends?
- Is there anything nice about ...?

- First of all, camping is cheaper. For example, ...
- Second, in my experience, ...
- Also, when I went camping, ...
- Furthermore, camping offers ...

- First, staying at a hotel is more convenient. For instance, ...
- If we stay at a hotel, we can ...
- Speaking of ..., hotels are better ...
- Moreover, ...

Decision Making ２人の部員の話をもとに、クラブ長は最終的な決断を下しましょう。部員Ａと部員Ｂの発言内容を簡単に振り返りながら、決断の理由を明確に示しましょう。

Leader's Decision	
結論	I decided to ( ) because A/B gave me a good reason.
まとめ・理由	・A/B said that _____ . ・The opinion was very persuasive to me. ・A/B's idea of ( ) is good, but _____ .

Review Your Role Play Role Play を振り返って、自分がどのように話したかをチェックしましょう。

Q1 順序立てて話したり、情報を追加したりするときの表現を使いましたか。
　□何度か使った　　□1回使った　　□使わなかった

Q2 Cue Expressionsやそれと同等の機能を持つ表現を使いましたか。
　□何度か使った　　□1回使った　　□使わなかった

Q3 メッセージを伝えるときに、いろいろな名詞句を使うことができましたか。
　□何度か使った　　□1回使った　　□使わなかった

Q4 自分の主張に対して、理由を明確に述べることができましたか。
　□複数の理由を述べた　　□1つの理由を述べた　　□理由を述べられなかった

Write Your Opinion

この章で学んだ語句を３つ以上使って、次のテーマについて100語以上のパラグラフを書きましょう。
⇨解答欄は p.130

Theme If you were the club leader, would you choose camping or staying at a hotel?

Further Activities

この章で学んだ内容に関連する情報を追加で調べ、クラスメイトとシェアしましょう。

Example 近年人気のキャンプ場やアウトドア活動について、調べてみましょう。

> Formulaic Expressions in Focus : **Asking for Clarification**

Unit 2

Which is better for your health, tea or coffee?

健康に良いのは
紅茶? コーヒー?

多くの人は紅茶やコーヒーを日常的に飲んでいます。これらを飲むことは私たちの健康にどのような効果があるのでしょうか。

Listen and *Interact*

1st Round Emma の意見に対する友達の意見を聞き、表にチェックを入れましょう。

Emma's opinion: I personally prefer drinking tea.

🎧 DL 05　💿 CD1-09

	Ray	Mina	Tim	Sophia
Prefers tea	☐	☐	☐	☐
Prefers coffee	☐	☐	☐	☐

2nd Round A. 次の表現の意味を確認し、音声に続いて声に出してみましょう。

B. 再度 *1st* Round の音声を聞き、使われている次の表現に○をつけましょう。

🎧 DL 06　💿 CD1-10

Formulaic Expressions　*Asking for Clarification*

📍 相手に発言を繰り返してもらいたいとき

Excuse me.　　Pardon me.　　Say that again, please.　　I beg your pardon?

Could you repeat ...?

📍 内容をもう少し説明してほしいとき

Can you tell me more about ...?　　What do you mean by ...?

I'm sorry, but I can't understand ...

17

1st *Round* の音声を聞いて下線部を埋めましょう。下線部は１語とは限りません。

Emma: People all over the world drink tea or coffee regularly. I personally prefer drinking tea because it's not too bitter. Ray, which do you prefer?

Ray: I drink both depending on my ¹_____. But if I had to choose one, I wouldn't choose coffee.

Emma: ²_____ that, Ray?

Ray: Oh, I'm saying I prefer tea. I like to choose various ³_____. What about you, Mina?

Mina: I definitely like coffee. I like its aroma.

Ray: ⁴_____, Mina.

Mina: Aroma! The unique smell of coffee beans makes me so ⁵_____. I like brewing it on my own with a dripper. How about you, Tim?

Tim: I am concerned about my health, so I prefer tea to coffee.

Mina: Oh, is tea healthier? Can you tell me more about that, Tim?

Tim: Well, tea has an anti-aging ⁶_____ that is good for your body. On top of that, it's easier to make tea than coffee—just ⁷_____ hot water into the teapot or into a cup with ⁸_____ in it. Which do you prefer, Sophia?

Sophia: I'd rather drink coffee. Coffee also has a chemical called polyphenol, which helps control ⁹_____. Also, by adding ¹⁰_____, drinking coffee becomes healthier.

Focus on **Sounds**

1st *Round* の音声を利用して、音読とシャドーイングを行いましょう。内容を理解しながら発音ポイントにも注意し、表に沿って５点満点で自己評価しましょう。

| 発音ポイント ❯ 語尾の子音 | People all over the world drink tea. [ℓ.1] |

※子音の後に母音を入れて発音しないように注意

音読 テキストを見ながら音読		内容・発音を意識して読めた度合い				
		5	4	3	2	1
パラレル音読 テキストを見ながら音声と同時に音読		内容・発音を意識して言えた度合い				
		5	4	3	2	1
シャドーイング テキストを見ないで音声の直後に復唱		ついていけた度合い				
		5	4	3	2	1

1. You can choose the type of beans.   **a | b**
2. It wakes you up because it has more caffeine.   **a | b**
3. You can add milk or lemon depending on your mood.   **a | b**
4. You can enjoy the nice aroma when you brew it from the beans.   **a | b**
5. You can prepare it just by putting a bag in a pot and pouring in hot water. **a | b**

Interaction これまでの内容を参考にして、下線部に語句を補いながら対話をしましょう。

A: Which is healthier, tea or coffee?

B: I think _____ is healthier.

A: **Can you tell me more about** your opinion?

B: Well, _____ has more / less caffeine, so it is good when ...

→ うまく言えなかった内容を英語でどう表現するか調べ、クラスメイトと共有しましょう。

Gather Information

Listening プレゼンテーションの音声を聞いてキーワードを書き取りましょう。

🎧 DL 07 ● CD1-11 ～ ● CD1-15

Facts

_____

_____

_____

Advantages of tea	**Advantages of coffee**

Which is better for your health, tea or coffee?

1　When you go to a café, what do you usually drink? Many would answer either tea or coffee. Needless to say, they are popular beverages worldwide. Their popularity could come from the positive effects on our bodies. Which do you think is better for health?

2　First, let's look at how tea and coffee became popular. Regarding tea, tea leaves are originally from East Asia. During the 18th century, black tea became popular as English tea all over the world through the colonization period. As for coffee, it was a kind of medicine in Arabia around the 10th century. By the 1600s, people were drinking it in the Middle East, Europe, and North America. It was imported to Japan in the 18th century by the Dutch.

3　Drinking tea has many advantages. First, tea has different flavors, which may positively affect your mental health. You can choose from different types of tea, such as Earl Grey, Orange Pekoe, or Darjeeling, to name a few. Since tea is easily made, you can choose whatever you want depending on your mood. Second, tea prevents you from catching the flu. It is said that you can lower your risk of infection by drinking tea daily. Third, tea has less caffeine and is rich in catechin. Unlike coffee, there is less danger of having too much caffeine per day. Tea catechin also has anti-aging effects. Drinking tea can keep your body young and healthy.

4　Coffee also has several advantages. First, roasted coffee has a nice aroma. When you smell the aroma, you can feel relaxed. Second, coffee includes caffeine which boosts your metabolism and keeps you wide-awake. When you feel tired or sleepy, you can feel refreshed by drinking coffee. Third, it is good for your skin. Coffee has polyphenol. This chemical helps your blood to circulate better, which can keep your skin healthy.

5　Both tea and coffee have an equal number of positive effects on health. While tea might be good for your mental health, coffee could support a more active

lifestyle. Because each option has various flavors, choosing which to drink depends on
30 your mood and preferences.   (354 words)

✎ **Notes**   catechin [kǽtəkin]「カテキン」 metabolism [mətǽbəlizəm]「(新陳) 代謝」
polyphenol [pɔ̀lifíːnɔl]「ポリフェノール」

🔍Focus on **Meaning**

本文の内容と一致するものはT、一致しないものはFを選びましょう。

1. People in Arabia in the 10th century drank coffee as a medicine.   T | F
2. People in Japan began to drink coffee in the 1600s.   T | F
3. If you drink tea often, you are less likely to catch a disease.   T | F
4. Drinking too much coffee is dangerous because it is rich in catechin.   T | F
5. Polyphenol increases your metabolism.   T | F

🔍Focus on **Vocabulary**

本文に登場する1〜5の語の同義語🟰または反意語↔として最も適切な語を選びましょう。

1. beverage   [ℓ.2] 🟰 dessert   meal   snack   drink
2. colonization [ℓ.6] ↔ being [settled   invaded   independent   royal]
3. import   [ℓ.8] ↔ deport   export   transport   report
4. infection   [ℓ.14] ↔ prevention   connection   negotiation   promotion
5. circulate   [ℓ.23] 🟰 block   operate   flow   leak

🔍Focus on **Grammar**   動詞と副詞

動詞に副詞を添えることによって、動作や状態をより正確に伝えることができます。
副詞が表す意味には頻度（always, usually, often, sometimesなど）や様態（well, fast,
silentlyなど）、程度（totally, almost, nearlyなど）などがあります。

例   What do you **usually drink**?
          副詞   動詞

   This chemical helps your blood to **circulate better**.
                                    動詞   副詞

📖 第3段落の動詞を修飾する副詞に下線を引き、意味を確認しましょう。
Task

Role Play Discussion

Situation を読み、3 人一組となっ
てそれぞれの役割に分かれディス
カッションをしましょう。メモは
キーワードレベルで準備し、右ペー
ジの表現例も参考にしながら、細
部は考えながら話しましょう。

Situation
スーパーマーケットの店長は、健康ブーム
の昨今、高齢者向けのセール品として紅茶
を仕入れるべきかコーヒーを仕入れるべき悩ん
でいます。店員Aは紅茶を、店員Bはコーヒーを
すすめています。店員の意見を聞き、店長はどち
らをセール品として仕入れるか決定しましょう。

Memo

Owner of a Supermarket	導入：I want to attract elderly customers by advertising tea or coffee at a discounted price. Which one should we promote more?

質問：

1. ....

2. ....

3. ....

Employee A	主張：I think we should promote tea more because it has three advantages.

例・理由：

1. ....

2. ....

3. ....

Employee B	主張：I think we should promote coffee more because it has three advantages.

例・理由：

1. ....

2. ....

3. ....

■ Do you drink coffee / tea every day?

■ Can you tell me more about ...?

■ What do you mean by ...?

■ I'm sorry but I can't understand ...

■ We should ...

■ First, drinking tea positively affects .... For example, ...

■ Second, ... In my experience, ...

■ Third, tea products will ...

■ We should ...

■ First, drinking coffee may be .... For example, my grandmother ...

■ Second, ... For instance, ...

■ Finally, coffee ...

Decision Making 2人の店員の話をもとに、店長は最終的な決断を下しましょう。店員Aと店員Bの発言内容を簡単に振り返りながら、決断の理由を明確に示しましょう。

	Owner's Decision
結論	I decided to promote ( ) more because A/B gave me a good reason.
まとめ・理由	・A/B said that _____ . ・The opinion was very persuasive to me. ・A/B's idea of ( ) is good, but _____ .

Review Your Role Play Role Playを振り返って、自分がどのように話したかをチェックしましょう。

Q1 相手に発言を繰り返してもらったり、もう少し説明してもらったりするときの表現を使いましたか。

☐ 何度か使った　　☐ 1回使った　　☐ 使わなかった

Q2 Cue Expressionsやそれと同等の機能を持つ表現を使いましたか。

☐ 何度か使った　　☐ 1回使った　　☐ 使わなかった

Q3 メッセージを伝えるときに、いろいろな動詞と副詞の組み合わせを使うことができましたか。

☐ 何度か使った　　☐ 1回使った　　☐ 使わなかった

Q4 自分の主張に対して、理由を明確に述べることができましたか。

☐ 複数の理由を述べた　　☐ 1つの理由を述べた　　☐ 理由を述べられなかった

Write Your Opinion

この章で学んだ語句を3つ以上使って、次のテーマについて100語以上のパラグラフを書きましょう。

⇨解答欄は p. 131

Theme If you were the owner of the supermarket, would you promote tea or coffee?

Further Activities

この章で学んだ内容に関連する情報を追加で調べ、クラスメイトとシェアしましょう。

Example 健康を維持するために世界で愛飲されているさまざまな飲み物には、どのようなものがあるでしょうか。

Unit 3

Which class style is more effective, face-to-face or online?

学習効果が高いのは
対面授業？ オンライン授業？

学生がオンライン授業を受ける機会は
年々増加しています。従来の対面授業と
オンライン授業では、学習効果に違いが
あるのでしょうか。

Listen and Interact

1st Round

Yota の意見に対する友達の意見を聞き、表にチェックを入れましょう。

Yota's opinion: I like face-to-face classes.

🎧 DL 08　　💿 CD1-16

	Sophia	Tim	Mina	Ray
Prefers face-to-face	☐	☐	☐	☐
Prefers online	☐	☐	☐	☐

2nd Round

A. 次の表現の意味を確認し、音声に続いて声に出してみましょう。

B. 再度 *1st* Round の音声を聞き、使われている次の表現に○をつけましょう。

🎧 DL 09　　💿 CD1-17

Formulaic Expressions　　*Agreeing with an Opinion*

📍 相手の発言に簡潔に同意するとき

Exactly!　　Definitely!　　Certainly!　　Precisely!

That's true.　　That's right.　　You're so right.

📍 相手の意見に強く同意するとき

I couldn't agree with you more.　　That's exactly how I see it.

You have a good point there.　　That's a very important point.

3rd Round 1st Roundの音声を聞いて下線部を埋めましょう。下線部は1語とは限りません。

Yota: We have various class styles at university now. I like face-to-face classes because I can see my friends on campus. Sophia, what's your opinion?

Sophia: Well, you have a good point there. But I actually think online classes ¹_____. You know, it's so nice to take classes at home. Also, you get ²_____ study time because you don't need to ³_____ to school. How about you, Tim?

Tim: ⁴_____, Sophia! I take the train to get to school, and it's always crowded in the morning. By the time I get to the campus, I'm already tired, and it's hard to ⁵_____. I also think online classes are more eco-friendly because almost all the learning materials are ⁶_____. Mina, which do you prefer?

Mina: Honestly, I prefer face-to-face classes. In addition to what Yota said, it's much easier to get teachers' help in the classroom than online. You ⁷_____ talk to them before or after class. There's no need to send an email to get an ⁸_____. Do you agree with me, Ray?

Ray: ⁹_____! It's easier to make a ¹⁰_____ for face-to-face classes. I love it because I don't forget to submit my weekly assignments!

🔍 Focus on Sounds

1st Roundの音声を利用して、音読とシャドーイングを行いましょう。内容を理解しながら発音ポイントにも注意し、表に沿って5点満点で自己評価しましょう。

発音ポイント ● 連続する子音　We ha**ve v**arious clas**s s**tyles. [ℓ.1]

音読 テキストを見ながら音読	内容・発音を意識して読めた度合い	
	5　4　3　2　1	
パラレル音読 テキストを見ながら音声と同時に音読	内容・発音を意識して言えた度合い	
	5　4　3　2　1	
シャドーイング テキストを見ないで音声の直後に復唱	ついていけた度合い	
	5　4　3　2　1	

Idea Generation 1〜5の文を読み、対面授業派（a）かオンライン授業派（b）かを判断しましょう。

1. Teachers can provide feedback in person.   a | b
2. You have more flexibility in your schedule.   a | b
3. You cannot take classes if your internet connection is unstable.   a | b
4. You can chat directly with your classmates in person after class.   a | b
5. Shy students may be able to participate in classes more actively.   a | b

Interaction これまでの内容を参考にして、下線部に語句を補いながら対話をしましょう。

A: Which class style do you think is more effective for students, face-to-face or online?

B: I think _____ classes are more effective. In my experience, _____.

A: That's exactly how I see it. Do you have any other reasons?

B: Well, when you take _____ classes, you can ...

→ うまく言えなかった内容を英語でどう表現するか調べ、クラスメイトと共有しましょう。

Gather Information

Listening プレゼンテーションの音声を聞いてキーワードを書き取りましょう。

DL 10   CD1-18 ~ CD1-22

Facts

_____

_____

_____

Advantages of face-to-face classes	Advantages of online classes

Face-to-face learning or online learning?

1 Recently, more university students get a chance to take online courses as technology advances. Some students learn better online, while others are more engaged in face-to-face classes. What are the advantages of the two learning styles from the students' viewpoint?

5 2 Online learning has been practiced worldwide in recent decades with more people having easy access to the Internet. Several studies show that online learning is as effective as face-to-face learning when comparing student performance. In addition, according to a survey conducted by the Japanese government in 2021, 56.9% of the students who have taken online classes were satisfied to some extent. However, during

10 the coronavirus pandemic, the government encouraged schools to have more face-to-face classes so that students would be able to experience real-world communication.

3 Face-to-face learning has two major advantages. First, there is natural interaction in class. Everyone—the teacher and students—is in the same classroom. When students have a question in class, they can directly ask their teacher or peers. Also, they can

15 work together in pairs or groups more easily. Another advantage is that students can maintain their concentration. With the physical presence of the teacher and classmates, students are less likely to get distracted during class.

4 On the other hand, the biggest advantage of online learning is its flexibility. Students can attend classes wherever they are. They might also be able to take classes at any

20 time if the teacher provides lecture videos or slides with audio online. Thus, students can balance their time between their studies and personal lives. In addition, students can learn more deeply. For example, with materials provided online, they can review the lessons as many times as they want

25 before submitting their assignments.

5 As you can see, both face-to-face and online learning styles have advantages. Obviously, some courses requiring physical contact with other students,

30　such as P.E. and science experiments, are not so suitable for online classes. Otherwise, which style is better depends on you. An ideal learning style is the one that meets your needs and priorities.

(337 words)

Focus on *Meaning*

本文の内容と一致するものはT、一致しないものはFを選びましょう。

1. More than half of the students feel unsatisfied with online classes.　　T | F
2. Students can ask questions more easily in a physical classroom.　　T | F
3. Face-to-face classes are distracting to students.　　T | F
4. Students have more control over their schedules by taking classes online.　　T | F
5. Online learning allows students to review the content of the lessons.　　T | F

Focus on *Vocabulary*

本文に登場する1〜5の語の同義語🔳または反意語🔁として最も適切な語を選びましょう。

1. viewpoint　[ℓ.4]　🔳　sight　stance　glance　grassroots
2. encourage　[ℓ.10]　🔁　block　bring　boost　belong
3. interaction　[ℓ.12]　🔳　connection　communication　imitation　participation
4. distracted　[ℓ.17]　🔁　alive　positive　focused　destroyed
5. assignment　[ℓ.25]　🔳　signature　similarity　stationery　homework

Focus on *Grammar*　　自動詞と他動詞

動詞には自動詞と他動詞の2種類があります。自動詞は目的語を必要としない動詞、他動詞は目的語を必要とする動詞です。自動詞・他動詞両方の使い方がある動詞もあります。動詞の用法と意味を把握することで、より正確にものごとを説明することができます。

例　Some students **learn** better online.
　　　　　　　　自動詞

More university students **get** a chance to take online courses.
　　　　　　　　　　　　他動詞　目的語

Task　第3段落の一般動詞に下線を引き、自動詞・他動詞どちらとして使われているか確認しましょう。

Role Play Discussion

Situation を読み、3人一組となっ
てそれぞれの役割に分かれディス
カッションをしましょう。メモは
キーワードレベルで準備し、右ペー
ジの表現例も参考にしながら、細
部は考えながら話しましょう。

Situation 3人の学生が、次学期の履修科目につい
て話し合っています。学生Aは、対面とオ
ンライン形式の両方がある講義についてどち
らを履修しようか迷っています。友達の学生Bは
対面形式を、学生Cはオンライン形式をすすめて
います。友達の意見を聞き、学生Aはどちらの形
式を履修するか決定しましょう。

 Student A

導入：I'm not sure if I should take the course on campus or online.
Which do you think is better?

質問：

1. ....

2. ....

3. ....

Student B

主張：I think you should take the course on campus. Let me give you
some reasons.

例・理由：

1. ....

2. ....

3. ....

Student C

主張：I suggest taking the course online. It has many advantages.

例・理由：

1. ....

2. ....

3. ....

- Do you think ...?
- Have you taken online lessons before?
- That's true.
- That's a very important point.

- First, according to the course syllabus, ...
- In my experience, face-to-face courses provide ...
- Also, ...
- In short, the face-to-face course ...

- First, this course is more suited to online study. For example, ...
- Second, ...
- I took some online courses last year, and ...
- If you take the course online, ...

Decision Making ２人の友達の話をもとに、学生 A は最終的な決断を下しましょう。学生 B と学生 C の発言内容を簡単に振り返りながら、決断の理由を明確に示しましょう。

	Student A's Decision
結論	I decided to take (　　　　　) because B/C gave me a good reason.
まとめ・理由	・B/C said that _____. ・The opinion was very persuasive to me. ・B/C's idea of (　　　　　) is good, but _____.

Review Your Role Play Role Play を振り返って、自分がどのように話したかをチェックしましょう。

Q1 相手の意見に同意するときの表現を使いましたか。

　　□何度か使った　　□１回使った　　□使わなかった

Q2 Cue Expressionsやそれと同等の機能を持つ表現を使いましたか。

　　□何度か使った　　□１回使った　　□使わなかった

Q3 メッセージを伝えるときに、自動詞や他動詞を意識して使うことができましたか。

　　□何度か使った　　□１回使った　　□使わなかった

Q4 自分の主張に対して、理由を明確に述べることができましたか。

　　□複数の理由を述べた　　□１つの理由を述べた　　□理由を述べられなかった

Write Your Opinion

この章で学んだ語句を３つ以上使って、次のテーマについて100語以上のパラグラフを書きましょう。　　　　　　　　　　　　　　　　　　　　　　⇨解答欄は p. 132

Theme　If you were Student A, would you take the course on campus or online?

Further Activities

この章で学んだ内容に関連する情報を追加で調べ、クラスメイトとシェアしましょう。

Example　国内外におけるオンライン授業の実践例について、具体的に調べてみましょう。

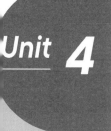
Unit 4
Which do you prefer, buying clothes or renting them?

服は買う派? レンタル派?

いろいろな服を着ておしゃれを楽しみたい人向けに、定額で流行の服を借りられるネットサービスがあります。従来の店舗で購入する形と比べて、メリットやデメリットを考えてみましょう。

Listen and *Interact*

 1st Round

Sophia の発言に対する友達の意見を聞き、表にチェックを入れましょう。

Sophia's statement: I'm thinking about using a clothing subscription site.

 DL 11   CD1-23

	Yota	Emma	Ray	Mina
Prefers buying clothes	☐	☐	☐	☐
Prefers renting clothes	☐	☐	☐	☐

2nd Round

A. 次の表現の意味を確認し、音声に続いて声に出してみましょう。

B. 再度 *1st* Round の音声を聞き、使われている次の表現に○をつけましょう。

 DL 12    CD1-24

Formulaic Expressions > *Expressing Partial Agreement / Polite Disagreement*

🔵 条件付きで賛成するとき

I partly agree.   My opinion is similar to ...   I mostly agree, but ...

I know what you want to say, but ...   I understand your point of view, but ...

🔵 丁寧に反対するとき

I'm sorry, but I can't agree.   I'm not sure about that.   Not necessarily.

I'm of a different opinion.

3rd Round 1st Round の音声を聞いて下線部を埋めましょう。下線部は1語とは限りません。

Sophia: I always want to wear fashionable clothes, so I'm thinking about using a clothing subscription site. I can rent a certain number of items per month at a fixed price. What do you think, Yota?

Yota: I think it's a great idea. I saw some high-end brands ¹_____ a rental service. The prices are ²_____, so you can save money. You can expect to pay only 10 to 20 percent of the ³_____. It's a pretty good deal. What do you say, Emma?

Emma: I partly agree with you, Yota, but I prefer buying my clothes. I want to look at real clothes in shops and ⁴_____ before buying them. On such subscription sites, you can see the sizes, but they are not always correct. Also, the color of the ⁵_____ on the computer screen is sometimes different from the actual item. What do you think, Ray?

Ray: I think you can save time by renting clothes. Instead of visiting many shops, you can take advantage of online catalogs and ⁶_____ a variety of new designs. Most rental services send the items in ⁷_____ days, so using a subscription site is an excellent idea!

Mina: I understand ⁸_____, but rental clothes are not always new. Even though they were dry-cleaned and ⁹_____, the condition may vary, and some could be ¹⁰_____ than you expected.

🔍 **Focus on Sounds**

1st Round の音声を利用して、音読とシャドーイングを行いましょう。内容を理解しながら発音ポイントにも注意し、表に沿って5点満点で自己評価しましょう。

発音ポイント ❥ [θ] [ð] [z] I'm **th**inking about u**s**ing a clo**th**ing subscription site. [ℓ.1~2]

音読 テキストを見ながら 音読	内容・発音を意識して読めた度合い				
	5	4	3	2	1
パラレル音読 テキストを見ながら 音声と同時に音読	内容・発音を意識して言えた度合い				
	5	4	3	2	1
シャドーイング テキストを見ないで 音声の直後に復唱	ついていけた度合い				
	5	4	3	2	1

34

Idea Generation 1〜5の文を読み、洋服を店舗で買う派（a）かネットでレンタルする派（b）かを判断しましょう。

1. You can save space in your closet.　　　　　　　　　　　　　a | b
2. You can save time by choosing clothes online.　　　　　　　a | b
3. You can actually try on different clothes at a shop.　　　　a | b
4. You can wear top designer brands for a lower price.　　　　a | b
5. You can meet friendly and knowledgeable shop assistants.　a | b

Interaction これまでの内容を参考にして、下線部に語句を補いながら対話をしましょう。

A: Which do you prefer, buying clothes or renting them?

B: I prefer _____ because _____. Don't you think so?

A: **I'm sorry, but I can't agree**. I think _____ because _____.

B: I know what you want to say, but ...

→ うまく言えなかった内容を英語でどう表現するか調べ、クラスメイトと共有しましょう。

Gather Information

Listening プレゼンテーションの音声を聞いてキーワードを書き取りましょう。

🎧 DL 13　CD1-25 ～ CD1-29

Facts

_____

_____

_____

Advantages of buying clothes	Advantages of renting clothes

Which do you prefer, buying clothes or renting them?

1 Some people love clothes and enjoy dressing up. However, shopping for new clothes is a burden on their budget. Even though most people still prefer to buy clothes, renting clothes for a monthly fee has become an option. Price competition among companies has made rental services more accessible for young people.

5 2 Traditionally, people only rented clothes for special occasions such as weddings and graduation ceremonies. However, recently many companies started to rent casual clothes for a fixed subscription price. In 2017, global sales of fashion subscriptions amounted to over one billion dollars. The trend of clothing rental services also matches a rising awareness of environmental issues. Over 500,000 tons of clothes are thrown
10 away every year in Japan. Many companies realized that sharing clothes can contribute to saving the planet.

3 However, many people still prefer buying clothes. First, you can enjoy shopping in physical shops. You can see the actual colors, touch the material, and try the clothes on. After buying them, you can wear them as long as you like. Second, you can take
15 your items home or even wear them immediately after your purchase. When you use rental services, you must wait for a while to receive your items. Third, there are shop assistants to answer your questions on the spot. If you cannot find exactly what you are looking for, they can give you some suggestions.

4 Conversely, some people are not necessarily for the idea of buying clothes. They
20 believe that there are advantages of clothing rental services. First, you can save money. For example, a company gives you the option of choosing as many items as you like for about 5,000 yen per month. Second, you can save space in your closet. Since you
25 have to return the items, renting clothes does not make you wonder where to store them. Third, you can try a variety of styles. Following an online stylist's advice, you can experiment with new styles.

30 　5　There are many ways to enjoy fashion, and both ways shown here have advantages. While many people will continue to shop at physical stores, the trend of clothing rental will surely change how we shop in the future.

(362 words)

Focus on **Meaning**

本文の内容と一致するものはT、一致しないものはFを選びましょう。

1. Renting clothes for special occasions is a recent trend.　　　　　　　　T｜F
2. Fashion subscriptions in Japan were worth more than one billion yen in 2017. T｜F
3. The fashion industry has started addressing environmental issues.　　　T｜F
4. The presence of a salesclerk is one of the benefits of in-store shopping.　T｜F
5. Renting clothes gives you opportunities to try new styles.　　　　　　　T｜F

Focus on **Vocabulary**

本文に登場する1〜5の語の同義語🟰または反意語⬄として最も適切な語を選びましょう。

1. competition　[ℓ.3]　⬄　completion　　cooperation　　interaction　　infection
2. occasion　　　[ℓ.5]　🟰　program　　performance　　celebrity　　celebration
3. awareness　　[ℓ.9]　🟰　consciousness　　happiness　　judgement　　movement
4. immediately　[ℓ.15]　⬄　earlier　　instantly　　later　　rapidly
5. store (v.)　　 [ℓ.26]　🟰　waste　　borrow　　shop　　keep

Focus on **Grammar**　　文型（SVOO・SVOC）

授与動詞（give, show, tellなど）を使って、与える対象（O₁）と与える物事（O₂）を目的語として2つ続けて言うことができます（SV O₁ O₂）。また、知覚動詞（see, feel, findなど）や使役動詞（make, have, letなど）を使って、対象（O）とその動き・状態など（C）を続けて言うことができます。Cには名詞、形容詞、動詞の原形などが使われます。

例　They can give you some suggestions.
　　S　　V　 O₁　　O₂

Price competition has made rental services more accessible for young people.
　　S　　　　V　　　O　　　　　C

Task　第4段落にあるSVOO・SVOCの文に下線を引き、意味を確認しましょう。

Role Play Discussion

Situation を読み、3人一組となってそれぞれの役割に分かれディスカッションをしましょう。メモはキーワードレベルで準備し、右ページの表現例も参考にしながら、細部は考えながら話しましょう。

Situation おしゃれを楽しみたい学生Aが、いろいろな服を着るために服を買い続けるか、定額のサブスクリプションサービスに加入するべきか悩んでいます。先輩の学生Bは購入を、学生Cはサブスクリプションをすすめています。先輩の意見を聞き、学生Aはどちらにするか決定しましょう。

Memo

Student A

導入：I am wondering whether I should start renting clothes. Which do you think is better, buying clothes or renting them? Tell me your opinion.

質問：

1. ....

2. ....

3. ....

Student B

主張：I recommend that you purchase your clothes. There are several advantages.

例・理由：

1. ....

2. ....

3. ....

Student C

主張：I recommend that you subscribe to a clothing rental service. It's great for the following reasons.

例・理由：

1. ....

2. ....

3. ....

Cue Expressions

■ How much do you spend each month on ...?
■ Do you often go ...?
■ What kind of ... do you like?
■ I mostly agree with you, but it's not necessarily true for me because ...

■ You should buy ...
■ For example, ...
■ I prefer to go to a store because ...
■ Seeing the clothes in the store lets you ...

■ I'm sorry, but I don't agree with you because ...
■ I have tried some subscription services, and ...
■ For instance, ...
■ I know what you want to say, but ...

Decision Making 2人の先輩の話をもとに、学生Aは最終的な決断を下しましょう。学生Bと学生Cの発言内容を簡単に振り返りながら、決断の理由を明確に示しましょう。

	Student A's Decision
結論	I decided to ( ) because B/C gave me a good reason.
まとめ・理由	・B/C said that _____. ・The opinion was very helpful to me. ・B/C's idea of ( ) is good, but _____.

 Review Your Role Play Role Play を振り返って、自分がどのように話したかをチェックしましょう。

Q1 条件付きで賛成する表現や丁寧に反対する表現を使うことができましたか。
☐ 何度か使った　　☐ 1回使った　　☐ 使わなかった

Q2 Cue Expressionsやそれと同等の機能を持つ表現を使いましたか。
☐ 何度か使った　　☐ 1回使った　　☐ 使わなかった

Q3 メッセージを伝えるときに、SVOO・SVOCの文型を使うことができましたか。
☐ 何度か使った　　☐ 1回使った　　☐ 使わなかった

Q4 自分の主張に対して、理由を明確に述べることができましたか。
☐ 複数の理由を述べた　　☐ 1つの理由を述べた　　☐ 理由を述べられなかった

Write Your Opinion

この章で学んだ語句を3つ以上使って、次のテーマについて100語以上のパラグラフを書きましょう。　　　　　　　　　　　　　　　　　　　　　　　⇨解答欄は p. 133

Theme If you were Student A, would you buy your clothes or subscribe to a rental service?

Further Activities

この章で学んだ内容に関連する情報を追加で調べ、クラスメイトとシェアしましょう。

Example ファッション業界が環境へ与えている影響について、調べてみましょう。

Unit 5

Should eSports be in the Olympic Games?

eスポーツが
オリンピック種目に?

コンピューターを使って対戦するeスポーツが人気になっています。オリンピック競技にすることについてどう考えますか。

Listen and *Interact*

1st Round

Timの質問に対する友達の意見を聞き、表にチェックを入れましょう。

Tim's question: Are eSports really sports?

🎧 DL 14　　◎ CD1-30

	Mina	Ray	Emma	Yota
Yes	☐	☐	☐	☐
No	☐	☐	☐	☐

2nd Round

A. 次の表現の意味を確認し、音声に続いて声に出してみましょう。

B. 再度 *1st Round* の音声を聞き、使われている次の表現に○をつけましょう。
但し、時制が異なる場合があります。

🎧 DL 15　　◎ CD1-31

Formulaic Expressions ▶ *Expressing Personal Opinions*

📍 自分の意見をやわらかく述べるとき

In my opinion, ...　　Personally, I believe / suppose / feel (that) ...

As far as I can see, ...　　It seems to me that ...　　Well, if you ask me, ...

📍 確信していることを述べるとき

I'm convinced that ...　　The point I'm trying to make is ...

My view / point of view is that ...　　The way I see it is that ...

3rd Round 1st Roundの音声を聞いて下線部を埋めましょう。下線部は1語とは限りません。

Tim: My high school had an eSports club. I kept wondering whether they were playing sports. ¹_____ that they were just playing video games. Are eSports really sports? What would you say, Mina?

Mina: ²_____, eSports are sports. In eSports games, you can be a boxer or a race car driver, for example. To be good at them, you need to practice how to ³_____ your body movements. What do you think, Ray?

Ray: ⁴_____, I believe hard physical training is an ⁵_____ _____ of any sport, such as running or basketball. In that sense, I would not say eSports are sports. How about you, Emma?

Emma: I understand how you feel, Ray, but ⁶_____ eSports are sports. The word "sport" has several meanings. It can mean ⁷_____ for fun. For example, chess is considered to be a sport. I hear it is ⁸_____ a sport by the International Olympic Committee. Yota, what do you think?

Yota: ⁹_____ eSports are still not sports. A sport should be something that can ¹⁰_____ your health physically and mentally. I've read an article about eSports players suffering from addiction.

✐*Note*   the International Olympic Committee (IOC) 「国際オリンピック委員会」

♪*Focus on Sounds*

1st Roundの音声を利用して、音読とシャドーイングを行いましょう。内容を理解しながら発音ポイントにも注意し、表に沿って5点満点で自己評価しましょう。

発音ポイント▶ [s] [ts]   My high school had an eSports club. [ℓ.1]

音読 テキストを見ながら音読		内容・発音を意識して読めた度合い				
		5	4	3	2	1
パラレル音読 テキストを見ながら音声と同時に音読		内容・発音を意識して言えた度合い				
		5	4	3	2	1
シャドーイング テキストを見ないで音声の直後に復唱		ついていけた度合い				
		5	4	3	2	1

42

Idea Generation 1〜5の文を読み、eSports をスポーツと呼ぶことに賛成派(a)か反対派(b)かを判断しましょう。

1. Sports should contribute to physical health.　　　　　　　　　a | b
2. You can improve your physical skills by playing eSports.　　　a | b
3. The definition of "sport" should be limited to physical activities.　a | b
4. Hard physical training should be required in sports.　　　　　a | b
5. The Olympic Committee should recognize eSports as official events.　a | b

Interaction これまでの内容を参考にして、下線部に語句を補いながら対話をしましょう。

A: Do you think eSports are sports?

B: **In my opinion**, eSports ＿＿＿＿＿＿ sports.

A: What's your definition of a sport?

B: **Personally**, **I believe** a sport should ...

↪ うまく言えなかった内容を英語でどう表現するか調べ、クラスメイトと共有しましょう。

Gather Information

Listening プレゼンテーションの音声を聞いてキーワードを書き取りましょう。

🎧 DL 16　💿 CD1-32 ～ 💿 CD1-36

Having eSports in the Olympics

Facts

For	Against

Should eSports be in the Olympic Games?

1 Have you ever played eSports? If you play online games, you probably have. eSports refer to competitions between players connected through video games. They are becoming popular around the world. Recently, it has been discussed whether eSports should be included in the Olympic Games. Do you think eSports belong there?

5 2 Most people think of sports as physical activities. However, the IOC recognizes a variety of activities as sports including chess and billiards. It may recognize eSports, too, and add them to the games because of their growing popularity. According to a report, eSports are expected to attract 577 million viewers by 2024. The question now is whether or not eSports should be played in the Olympic Games.

10 3 Let's look at the opinions of people who want eSports in the Olympics. First, many young people enjoy playing eSports. If they become an Olympic sport, fans would be excited to watch top players from various countries. Second, eSports do not cost as much as some traditional sports. They do not require large fields or facilities. Third, eSports are sports that require the integration of various skills like quick reflexes, 15 concentration, and imagination. They are not much different from sports recognized as Olympic events today.

4 Now, let's go over concerns about adding eSports to the Olympics. To begin with, eSports may negatively influence players' health. Young children in particular may play video games for a long time and become addicted to them, even resulting in death. Aside 20 from those extreme cases, parents worry that their children will spend hours or days in a seat without sleeping or getting any exercise. Moreover, some games are violent. In those games, players kill creatures or fight with weapons. Many argue that such 25 games should be banned since the Olympics are a festival of peace.

5 Summing up, eSports are growing in popularity. Including the new sports in

the Olympics will surely make the event more attractive to younger generations. At
the same time, some people find eSports unacceptable. They are not comfortable with
adding them to the Olympic Games. Which side would you support?   (347 words)

30

✐*Note*   reflexes「反射神経」

⌕*Focus on* **Meaning**

本文の内容と一致するものはT、一致しないものはFを選びましょう。

1. eSports refer to competitions to create video games.   T｜F
2. The IOC recognizes activities with little physical movement as sports.   T｜F
3. eSports are more economical than some sports.   T｜F
4. Some people oppose eSports because they can be bad for one's health.   T｜F
5. eSports can increase the popularity of the Olympics for older generations.   T｜F

⌕*Focus on* **Vocabulary**

本文に登場する1〜5の語句の同義語🟰または反意語↔として最も適切な語を選びましょう。

1. refer to   [ℓ.2]   🟰   deny   mean   reflect   refuse
2. recognize   [ℓ.5]   🟰   neglect   notice   respond   record
3. integration   [ℓ.14] ↔   being [assembled   combined   separated   squeezed]
4. concern   [ℓ.17] 🟰   claim   request   suggestion   anxiety
5. addicted   [ℓ.19] ↔   indifferent   interested   poisoned   playful

⌕*Focus on* **Grammar**   助動詞

助動詞 (will, can, may, must, shall, would, could, might, ought to, shouldなど) を使
い分けることによって、動詞で示す内容に、可能性・確信・意思・評価などの度合
いを加えることができます。

例 It has been discussed whether eSports **should** be included in the Olympic
Games.
It **may** recognize eSports, too, and add them to the games.

📖
Task   第4段落の助動詞に下線を引き、意味を確認しましょう。

Role Play Discussion

Situation を読み、3人一組となってそれぞれの役割に分かれディスカッションをしましょう。メモはキーワードレベルで準備し、右ページの表現例も参考にしながら、細部は考えながら話しましょう。

Situation オリンピックの開催都市には、実施競技の提案権があります。開催都市のリーダーが、eスポーツを提案するべきか悩んでいます。同僚Aは賛成、同僚Bは反対の立場を取っています。同僚の意見を聞き、リーダーはeスポーツを提案するかどうかを決定しましょう。

Memo 🖉

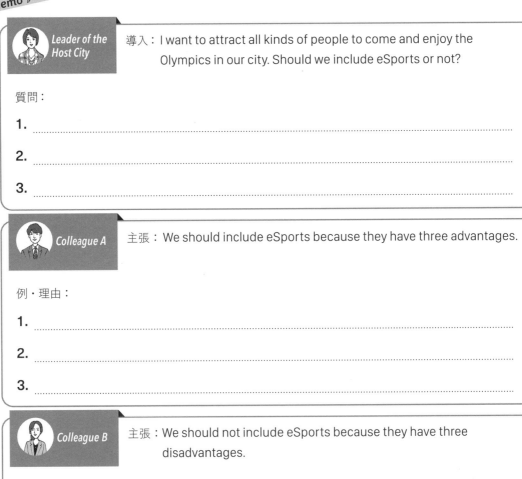

Leader of the Host City

導入：I want to attract all kinds of people to come and enjoy the Olympics in our city. Should we include eSports or not?

質問：

1. ....
2. ....
3. ....

Colleague A

主張：We should include eSports because they have three advantages.

例・理由：

1. ....
2. ....
3. ....

Colleague B

主張：We should not include eSports because they have three disadvantages.

例・理由：

1. ....
2. ....
3. ....

■ What are some advantages and disadvantages of ...?
■ Can you tell me ...?
■ Will many people find eSports ...?
■ As far as I can see, ...

■ In my opinion, we should ...
■ First, eSports enable .... For example, ...
■ Second, ... I read an article ...
■ In sum, eSports can / may / would ...

■ I'm convinced that eSports ...
■ For one thing, many people worry .... To give an example, ...
■ Another point is .... It is often said ...
■ To sum up, eSports can / may / would ...

Decision Making　2人の同僚の話をもとに、リーダーは最終的な決断を下しましょう。同僚Aと同僚Bの発言内容を簡単に振り返りながら、決断の理由を明確に示しましょう。

	Leader's Decision
結論	I decided (to / not to) include eSports in the Olympics because A/B gave me a good reason.
まとめ・理由	・A/B said that _____ . ・The opinion was very persuasive to me. ・A/B's idea of ( ) is good, but _____ .

Review Your Role Play　Role Play を振り返って、自分がどのように話したかをチェックしましょう。

Q1　自分の意見や確信していることを述べるときの表現を使いましたか。

　　□ 何度か使った　　□ 1回使った　　□ 使わなかった

Q2　Cue Expressionsやそれと同等の機能を持つ表現を使いましたか。

　　□ 何度か使った　　□ 1回使った　　□ 使わなかった

Q3　メッセージを伝えるときに、助動詞を意識して使うことができましたか。

　　□ 何度か使った　　□ 1回使った　　□ 使わなかった

Q4　自分の主張に対して、理由を明確に述べることができましたか。

　　□ 複数の理由を述べた　　□ 1つの理由を述べた　　□ 理由を述べられなかった

Write Your Opinion

この章で学んだ語句を３つ以上使って、次のテーマについて100語以上のパラグラフを書きましょう。　　　　　　　　　　　　　　　　　　　　　　　　⇨解答欄は p. 134

Theme　If you were the leader of the host city, would you include eSports in the Olympics?

Further Activities

この章で学んだ内容に関連する情報を追加で調べ、クラスメイトとシェアしましょう。

Example　近年追加されたオリンピック種目には、どのようなものがあるでしょうか。

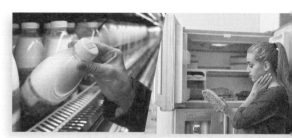

Unit 6

Should food companies abandon best-before dates?

食品ロス削減のために賞味期限表示をなくすべきか？

食品ロスの観点から、食品の期限表示の是非が世界的に話題になっています。賞味期限表示の廃止は食品ロスの削減につながるのでしょうか。

Listen and *Interact*

1st Round

Mina の意見に対する友達の意見を聞き、表にチェックを入れましょう。

Mina's opinion: Food companies should abandon best-before dates.

🎧 DL 17　　💿 CD1-37

	Tim	Sophia	Yota	Emma
Agrees	☐	☐	☐	☐
Disagrees	☐	☐	☐	☐

2nd Round

A. 次の表現の意味を確認し、音声に続いて声に出してみましょう。

B. 再度 *1st Round* の音声を聞き、使われている次の表現に○をつけましょう。

🎧 DL 18　　💿 CD1-38

Formulaic **Expressions**　*Giving Reasons or Evidence*

📍 **主張の理由を述べるとき**

As ..., ...　　Since ..., ...　　Because ..., ...　　Due to ..., ...　　Because of ..., ...

Owing to ..., ...　　Given that ..., ...　　The reason (for this) is ...

I tell you all this because ...

📍 **主張の根拠を述べるとき**

According to ..., ...　　I base my argument on ...

Research / Evidence shows that ...　　From what I've read, ...

3rd Round　1st Roundの音声を聞いて下線部を埋めましょう。下線部は1語とは限りません。

Mina: How can we reduce food waste? I think food companies should abandon best-before dates. What do you think, Tim?

Tim: I couldn't agree with you more. ¹_____, most processed food tastes fine even after the best-before dates. Also, ²_____ _____, it's totally fine to use ³_____ to check if the food is still safe. What do you think, Sophia?

Sophia: Isn't it ⁴_____ to do that? Since most of us aren't specialists in food safety, we may ⁵_____ whether the food is good or bad. So, I'm against that idea. What's your opinion, Yota?

Yota: I'm with you, Sophia, but for different reasons. I think abandoning best-before dates would cause more food waste. ⁶_____ because people don't usually pay attention to when they buy food. Best-before dates prevent people from ⁷_____ food too soon. What do you think, Emma?

Emma: Well, the other day I attended a presentation given by a ⁸_____ _____. She insisted that consumers take ⁹_____ for what and how much food they buy and eat. Without best-before dates, we have to keep track of the food we store at home. The more we think about food ¹⁰_____, the more we can reduce food waste.

🔍 Focus on *Sounds*

1st Roundの音声を利用して、音読とシャドーイングを行いましょう。内容を理解しながら発音ポイントにも注意し、表に沿って5点満点で自己評価しましょう。

発音ポイント ▶ [f] [v] [b]　Most processed **f**ood tastes **f**ine e**v**en a**f**ter the **b**est-**b**efore dates.

[ℓ.3~4]

音読 テキストを見ながら音読		内容・発音を意識して読めた度合い				
		5	4	3	2	1
パラレル音読 テキストを見ながら音声と同時に音読		内容・発音を意識して言えた度合い				
		5	4	3	2	1
シャドーイング テキストを見ないで音声の直後に復唱		ついていけた度合い				
		5	4	3	2	1

50

Idea Generation 1〜5の文を読み、賞味期限表示の廃止に賛成派(a)か反対派(b)かを判断しましょう。

1. Consumers can judge the freshness by themselves.   a | b
2. Food is thrown away too quickly due to best-before dates.   a | b
3. Less food is wasted when best-before dates are not displayed.   a | b
4. Best-before dates help consumers choose fresh food in the store.   a | b
5. With best-before dates, consumers can judge when to throw away the food.   a | b

Interaction これまでの内容を参考にして、下線部に語句を補いながら対話をしましょう。

A: Should food companies abandon best-before dates?

B: Yes, they should. / No, they shouldn't. **The reason is** _____ .

A: Can you tell me more about your opinion?

B: Well, **according to** ...

→ うまく言えなかった内容を英語でどう表現するか調べ、クラスメイトと共有しましょう。

Gather Information

Listening プレゼンテーションの音声を聞いてキーワードを書き取りましょう。

🎧 DL 19   💿 CD1-39 ~ 💿 CD1-43

Abandoning best-before dates

Facts

_____

_____

_____

Advantages	**Disadvantages**

Should food companies abandon best-before dates?

1 Did you know that there are two types of date labeling on foods? One is the use-by date, showing the time until when the food is safe to eat. The other is the best-before date, showing the time until when the food tastes or looks good. Recently, the latter has been an issue related to food waste. Is abandoning best-before dates a good idea?

2 To begin with, let's learn the history of food safety. Japan began labeling manufactured-on dates in 1948. The rule was then changed in 1995 to meet international standards. Since then, best-before and use-by dates have been adopted instead. However, according to a study conducted by the European Commission in 2018, this international rule is estimated to cause up to 10% of the annual food waste in the EU. Unlike the use-by dates, the best-before dates do not indicate that the food is unsafe after the date. Would abandoning best-before dates help solve some food waste issues?

3 There are two main advantages to abandoning best-before dates. First, it can prevent food waste in the distribution process. The Japanese food industry has a particular practice: when shipping products, food manufacturers make sure that the best-before dates are later than the dates of already shipped products. This forces the manufacturers to dispose of "older products" in stock. Those products could still be distributed if the dates were not printed on the labels. Second, abandoning best-before dates can help reduce food waste at home. Given that there is no date to rely on, consumers can use their senses and knowledge to judge if the food is safe.

4 Abandoning best-before dates also has two possible drawbacks. First, it may actually cause more food waste. Most people live busy lives, so they cannot necessarily remember when they bought the food. This may make consumers throw away more food. Second, consumers may be exposed to health risks such as food poisoning. To protect themselves, consumers must rely on their own knowledge of food safety.

30 **5** Clearly, labeling best-before dates has both positive and negative effects. In order to decide whether we should allow food companies to abandon them, we need to understand the importance of food safety control as well as various causes of food waste.

(374 words)

✐*Notes*   use-by date「消費期限」 manufactured-on date「製造年月日」
the European Commission「欧州委員会」

Focus on **Meaning**

本文の内容と一致するものはT、一致しないものはFを選びましょう。

1. Best-before dates show the last day when you can eat the food safely.   T | F
2. Date labeling on foods started in 1995 in Japan.   T | F
3. One practice of the Japanese food industry may create food waste.   T | F
4. People can decide when to throw away the food if dates are not shown.   T | F
5. Date labeling is one of the causes of food poisoning.   T | F

Focus on **Vocabulary**

本文に登場する1〜5の語の同義語▤または反意語⬌として最も適切な語を選びましょう。

1. meet	[ℓ.7]	▤	annoy	offend	fail	match
2. distribution	[ℓ.14]	▤	direction	delivery	penalty	prime
3. practice	[ℓ.15]	▤	custom	proverb	research	solution
4. dispose	[ℓ.17]	⬌	call	drive	send	keep
5. expose	[ℓ.26]	⬌	collect	hint	protect	waste

Focus on **Grammar**   受け身の表現

受け身の表現を使うと、人などの動作主よりもその動作の影響を受ける側に焦点をあてることができます。また、受け身の形は助動詞とともに用いたり、完了形や進行形と組み合わせたりしてさまざまなメッセージを伝えることができます。

例 The rule **was changed** in 1995.
Best-before and use-by dates **have been adopted** instead.

Task 第3段落にある受け身の表現に下線を引き、意味を確認しましょう。

Role Play Discussion

Situation を読み、3人一組となっ
てそれぞれの役割に分かれディス
カッションをしましょう。メモは
キーワードレベルで準備し、右ペー
ジの表現例も参考にしながら、細
部は考えながら話しましょう。

Situation

食品会社の社長が、食品ロスを減らすため
に賞味期限表示を廃止するべきか考えていま
す。従業員Aは廃止に賛成、従業員Bは反対の意
見を持っています。従業員の意見を聞き、社長は
廃止の是非を決定しましょう。

CEO of a Food Manufacturing Company

導入：We have to contribute to reducing food waste. Should our company abandon best-before dates?

質問：

1. ....

2. ....

3. ....

Employee A

主張：I think we should abandon best-before dates. It has some advantages.

例・理由：

1. ....

2. ....

3. ....

Employee B

主張：I don't think we should abandon best-before dates. Let me tell you why.

例・理由：

1. ....

2. ....

3. ....

54

■ What makes you believe ...?

■ Tell me the reasons why you ...

■ Can you share your experience with ...?

■ According to ...

■ First of all, best-before dates are labelled because ...

■ Research shows that ...

■ Our company can ...

■ Therefore, keeping best-before dates will ...

■ First, if we keep best-before dates, ...

■ Given that people tend to ...

■ From what I've read, ...

■ Thus, abandoning best-before dates will ...

Decision Making ２人の従業員の話をもとに、社長は最終的な決断を下しましょう。従業員Ａと従業員Ｂの発言内容を簡単に振り返りながら、決断の理由を明確に示しましょう。

	CEO's Decision
結論	I decided (to / not to) abandon best-before dates because A/B gave me a good reason.
まとめ・理由	・A/B said that _____. ・The opinion was very persuasive to me. ・A/B's idea of ( ) is good, but _____.

 Review Your Role Play Role Play を振り返って、自分がどのように話したかをチェックしましょう。

Q1 主張の理由や根拠を述べるときの表現を使いましたか。

    □ 何度か使った   □ 1回使った   □ 使わなかった

Q2 Cue Expressionsやそれと同等の機能を持つ表現を使いましたか。

    □ 何度か使った   □ 1回使った   □ 使わなかった

Q3 メッセージを伝えるときに、受け身の表現を使うことができましたか。

    □ 何度か使った   □ 1回使った   □ 使わなかった

Q4 自分の主張に対して、理由を明確に述べることができましたか。

    □ 複数の理由を述べた   □ 1つの理由を述べた   □ 理由を述べられなかった

Write Your Opinion

この章で学んだ語句を３つ以上使って、次のテーマについて100語以上のパラグラフを書きましょう。

⇨解答欄は p. 135

Theme If you were the CEO, would you abandon best-before dates?

Further Activities

この章で学んだ内容に関連する情報を追加で調べ、クラスメイトとシェアしましょう。

Example 食品ロスを削減するために国内外で行われている活動について、具体的に調べてみましょう。

Unit 7

Where do you like to watch movies, at a theater or at home?

映画を見るなら
映画館派? 自宅派?

多くの人が趣味や娯楽として映画鑑賞を
楽しんでいます。映画館での鑑賞と自宅
での鑑賞には、それぞれどのような良さ
があるのでしょうか。

Listen and Interact

 1st Round

Rayの意見に対する友達の意見を聞き、表にチェックを入れましょう。

Ray's opinion: I like watching movies at home.

 🎧 DL 20   ◉ CD1-44

	Emma	Yota	Sophia	Tim
Prefers a theater	☐	☐	☐	☐
Prefers home	☐	☐	☐	☐

 2nd Round

A. 次の表現の意味を確認し、音声に続いて声に出してみましょう。

B. 再度 *1st* Roundの音声を聞き、使われている次の表現に○をつけましょう。

 🎧 DL 21   ◉ CD1-45

Formulaic Expressions ⟩ *Paraphrasing an Idea*

● 自分の発言を言い換えるとき

That is, ...   I mean, ...   In other words, ...

To put it another way, ...   What I'm trying to say is ...

● 相手の発言内容を確認するとき

So, are you saying that ...?   Am I correct in understanding that ...?

Let me summarize what you have said.

3rd Round 1st Roundの音声を聞いて下線部を埋めましょう。下線部は1語とは限りません。

Ray: Many people like going to see movies. But I myself like watching movies at home because I can watch them anytime I want to. Emma, what's your opinion?

Emma: Well, I don't often watch movies, but when I do, I prefer going to a theater. Watching movies is something special to me.

Ray: [1]_____ you like the special [2]_____ at a theater?

Emma: That's right, Ray. Some theaters even have seats that move. What do you think, Yota?

Yota: I know what you mean by "feeling [3]_____" at a theater. However, at home, you can watch movies while you're relaxed and comfortable in [4]_____. To me, that's more important. What about you, Sophia?

Sophia: I have no problem with [5]_____, but I think movie nights at home are the best because everything is under my control. I mean, you can [6]_____ the movie anytime, and you can have any kinds of drinks or food [7]_____. Don't you think that's great, Tim?

Tim: I do [8]_____, but I think the image quality and [9]_____ are the most important. That is, you can watch movies on a big screen at a theater with excellent sound quality. It's so amazing that you can't [10]_____ what you have at home.

🔍 *Focus on* **Sounds**

1st Roundの音声を利用して、音読とシャドーイングを行いましょう。内容を理解しながら発音ポイントにも注意し、表に沿って5点満点で自己評価しましょう。

発音ポイント▶ [w] [ou] I myself like **w**atching movies at h**o**me. [ℓ.1]

音読 テキストを見ながら 音読		内容・発音を意識して読めた度合い 5　4　3　2　1	
パラレル音読 テキストを見ながら 音声と同時に音読		内容・発音を意識して言えた度合い 5　4　3　2　1	
シャドーイング テキストを見ないで 音声の直後に復唱		ついていけた度合い 5　4　3　2　1	

1～5の文を読み、映画館派(a)か自宅派(b)かを判断しましょう。

1. Setting up a home theater may cost a lot.　　　　　　　　　a | b
2. People around you are sometimes too noisy.　　　　　　　　a | b
3. You can start watching a movie whenever you want to.　　　a | b
4. It gives you an opportunity to go out with your friends.　　a | b
5. You can watch movies on your smartphone or tablet computer.　a | b

Interaction これまでの内容を参考にして、下線部に語句を補いながら対話をしましょう。

A: Where do you like to watch movies, at a theater or at home?
B: I think ＿＿＿＿＿＿ is better because ＿＿＿＿＿.
A: **So, are you saying** ＿＿＿＿＿?
B: Sure. **To put it another way**, ...

→うまく言えなかった内容を英語でどう表現するか調べ、クラスメイトと共有しましょう。

Gather Information

Listening プレゼンテーションの音声を聞いてキーワードを書き取りましょう。

🎧 DL 22　◉ CD1-46 ～ ◉ CD1-50

Watching movies

Facts

Advantages of watching at a theater	Advantages of watching at home

Reading 次の英文を読んで、内容を理解しましょう。後の設問にも答えましょう。

🎧 DL 22　◉ CD1-46 ～ ◉ CD1-50

Watching movies at a theater or at home?

1　Today, there are many choices of where to watch movies. We can enjoy movies not only at a theater but also at home. Some people have strong feelings about which place is better for watching movies.

2　The ways people watch movies have been changing. The Motion Picture Association did research worldwide on that matter from 2016 to 2020. According to the results, the percentage of people watching movies through digital services increased from 30% in 2016 to 48% in 2019, while the percentage of people going to theaters declined from 51% to 43%. Focusing on Japan, a survey conducted in 2018 shows that only 35% of the respondents visited theaters in that year. However, about half of those who did not visit a theater watched movies somewhere else. This indicates that more people watched movies somewhere other than a theater, possibly at home.

3　Even so, some people still strongly prefer going to theaters for many reasons. First, thanks to the equipment at a theater, moviegoers can enjoy high-quality images and great sound effects. Second, theaters usually show the latest movies, so people can keep themselves up to date on current trends. Third, watching a movie can be a social event. Theaters are often located in commercial areas, that is, places with lots of shops and restaurants. Thus, you can eat or shop with your friends before and after watching a movie.

4　With regard to watching movies at home, people often point out three advantages. First, it is more convenient. For example, if you need a restroom break or want to get more drinks or food, you can pause the movie at any time. Second, these days, it is not hard to set up a customized home theater. Electronics stores offer many choices of high-resolution screens and high-quality sound systems. Finally, viewers can access a huge selection of movies. Digital subscription services continually update their catalogs, so viewers have almost unlimited choices to choose from.

30 **5** In short, for watching movies, both theaters and your own home have advantages. Which you choose depends on your preferences; in other words, you can decide based on what is important to you.

(356 words)

✍ *Note*   the Motion Picture Association「映画協会」

⌕*Focus on* **Meaning**

本文の内容と一致するものはT、一致しないものはFを選びましょう。

1. The number of people going to theaters has been increasing.　　　　T｜F
2. You can keep up with new releases by going to the theater.　　　　T｜F
3. Going to the theater is a good way to hang out with your friends.　　T｜F
4. It is possible to build a home theater with quality equipment.　　　T｜F
5. The selection of movies you can watch at home is highly limited.　　T｜F

⌕*Focus on* **Vocabulary**

本文に登場する1〜5の語の同義語**≡**または反意語**⇔**として最も適切な語句を選びましょう。

1. matter　　[ℓ.5]　**≡**　news　　issue　　saying　　industry
2. respondent　[ℓ.9]　**≡**　a person who [accepts　ignores　replies　rejects]
3. equipment　[ℓ.13]　**≡**　devices　　vending machines　　lavatory　　staff
4. commercial　[ℓ.16]　**⇔**　residential　　downtown　　industrial　　busy
5. customize　　[ℓ.22]　**⇔**　to make things [distinctive　common　unique　special]

⌕*Focus on* **Grammar**　　重文と複文

重文を作る等位接続詞（and, but, so など）や、複文を作る従属接続詞（if, because, when, while など）を使って、より複雑な内容を表すことができます。

例　Theaters usually show the latest movies, **so** people can keep themselves up to date.［重文］

　　The percentage of people watching movies through digital services increased in 2019, **while** the percentage of people going to theaters declined.［複文］

Task　第4段落の重文・複文に下線を引き、それぞれが重文か複文かを確認しましょう。

Role Play Discussion

Situation を読み、3人一組となっ
てそれぞれの役割に分かれディス
カッションをしましょう。メモは
キーワードレベルで準備し、右ペー
ジの表現例も参考にしながら、細
部は考えながら話しましょう。

Situation

　　3人の学生たちが次の週末の予定を立て
ています。映画鑑賞をしようと提案した学
生Aは鑑賞方法について迷っています。友達の学
生Bは映画館で、学生Cは誰かの自宅での映画鑑
賞をすすめています。友達の意見を聞き、学生A
はどちらにするか決定しましょう。

Memo

Student A

導入：Let's watch a movie this weekend. Where should we watch it, at a theater or at one of our homes?

質問：

1. ....
2. ....
3. ....

Student B

主張：Watching movies at a theater is better for many reasons.

例・理由：

1. ....
2. ....
3. ....

Student C

主張：Watching movies at home is better for many reasons.

例・理由：

1. ....
2. ....
3. ....

Cue Expressions

- What is good about ...?
- Do you often watch movies at ...?
- Why do you do so?
- Let me summarize what you have said.

- A theater is better for watching movies because ...
- First, you can ...
- I mean, when I go to the theater, ...
- So, let's go to the theater and ...

- Home is better for watching movies because ...
- For example, you can ...
- In other words, a home theater is ...
- For these reasons, I definitely think ...

２人の友達の話をもとに、学生Aは最終的な決断を下しましょう。学生Bと学生Cの発言内容を簡単に振り返りながら、決断の理由を明確に示しましょう。

	Student A's Decision
結論	Let's watch a movie at (　　　　　　　　) because B/C gave me a good reason.
まとめ・理由	・B/C said that _____. ・The opinion was very appealing to me. ・B/C's idea of (　　　　　) is good, but _____.

 Role playを振り返って、自分がどのように話したかをチェックしましょう。

Q1 自分の発言を言い換えたり、相手の発言内容を確認したりするときの表現を使いましたか。
　　　☐何度か使った　　　☐1回使った　　　☐使わなかった

Q2 Cue Expressionsやそれと同等の機能を持つ表現を使いましたか。
　　　☐何度か使った　　　☐1回使った　　　☐使わなかった

Q3 メッセージを伝えるときに、重文や複文を意識して使うことができましたか。
　　　☐何度か使った　　　☐1回使った　　　☐使わなかった

Q4 自分の主張に対して、理由を明確に述べることができましたか。
　　　☐複数の理由を述べた　　　☐1つの理由を述べた　　　☐理由を述べられなかった

Write Your Opinion

この章で学んだ語句を３つ以上使って、次のテーマについて100語以上のパラグラフを書きましょう。
⇨解答欄は p. 136

Theme If you were Student A, would you watch a movie with your friends at a theater or at home?

Further Activities

この章で学んだ内容に関連する情報を追加で調べ、クラスメイトとシェアしましょう。

Example 現在人気の動画のサブスクリプションサービスや映画館には、どのようなものがあるでしょうか。

Unit 8 *Should homeowners install solar panels?*

個人宅にもソーラーパネルを
設置すべきか？

二酸化炭素を排出しない発電法として
太陽光発電が注目されています。個人宅
にもソーラーパネルを設置するべきで
しょうか。

Listen and **Interact**

 1st Round Emma の意見に対する友達の意見を聞き、表にチェックを入れましょう。

Emma's opinion: Homeowners should install solar panels on their roofs.

 DL 23  CD2-02

	Mina	Ray	Tim	Sophia
Agrees	☐	☐	☐	☐
Disagrees	☐	☐	☐	☐

 2nd Round **A.** 次の表現の意味を確認し、音声に続いて声に出してみましょう。

B. 再度 *1st Round* の音声を聞き、使われている次の表現に○をつけましょう。

 DL 24  CD2-03

Formulaic Expressions *Asking for Opinions*

🔵 相手に話すきっかけを与えるとき

What do you think about / of ...?　　Could you tell me ...?

How do you feel about ...?　　May I ask you ...?

🔵 相手からの情報を求めるとき

Can you think of an example?　　What's your opinion about ...?

Do you have any thoughts on ...?

Do you happen to know whether or not ...?

Emma: I see many houses with solar panels on their roofs these days. I think more homeowners should install them. This is a good ¹＿＿＿＿＿＿＿, isn't it, Mina?

Mina: ²＿＿＿＿＿＿＿＿! Those black panels are ³＿＿＿＿＿. I have always wanted to live in a house with a colorful roof. Solar panels cover most of the roof. ⁴＿＿＿＿＿＿＿＿＿＿＿＿＿＿＿ the color of the panels, Ray?

Ray: I don't think it's important, Mina. Solar panels can help people save on ⁵＿＿＿＿＿＿＿＿＿＿. Energy prices have been on the rise recently. On top of that, solar panels are a good source of ⁶＿＿＿＿＿＿＿＿＿＿. No carbon dioxide is emitted as they produce electricity. Tim, could you tell me your idea?

Tim: Sure. I personally feel solar panels will help us ⁷＿＿＿＿＿＿＿＿＿＿＿. Do you remember the blackout the other day because of the typhoon? If we have solar panels on our roofs, ⁸＿＿＿＿＿＿＿＿＿＿ electricity at home. Sophia, what do you think about this?

Sophia: You may be right, but I am a bit ⁹＿＿＿＿＿＿＿＿＿＿ solar panels at the moment. I hear we can't expect a steady supply of electricity ¹⁰＿＿＿＿＿ ＿＿＿＿＿＿＿, for example. For now, installing solar panels is a waste of money.

ⓒFocus on Sounds

1st *Round*の音声を利用して、音読とシャドーイングを行いましょう。内容を理解しながら発音ポイントにも注意し、表に沿って５点満点で自己評価しましょう。

発音ポイント ▶ [s] [z] [ð] I **s**ee many hou**s**e**s** wi**th s**olar panel**s** on **th**eir roof**s th**ese day**s**. [ℓ.1]

音読 テキストを見ながら音読		内容・発音を意識して読めた度合い				
		5	4	3	2	1
パラレル音読 テキストを見ながら音声と同時に音読		内容・発音を意識して言えた度合い				
		5	4	3	2	1
シャドーイング テキストを見ないで音声の直後に復唱		ついていけた度合い				
		5	4	3	2	1

Idea Generation 1～5の文を読み、ソーラーパネルの個人宅設置に賛成派(a)か反対派(b)かを判断しましょう。

1. People can have a power source even in a blackout.　　　　　a | b
2. Installing solar panels can provide financial benefits.　　　　a | b
3. Bad weather can prevent us from getting enough electricity.　a | b
4. Houses with solar panels will affect the landscape negatively.　a | b
5. Electricity generated by solar panels is environmentally friendly.　a | b

Interaction これまでの内容を参考にして、下線部に語句を補いながら対話をしましょう。

A: Do you think homeowners should install solar panels?

B: Personally, I feel they should / shouldn't.

A: Could you tell me why you think that way?

B: Well, if we install solar panels on our roofs, we ＿＿＿＿＿＿. …

→うまく言えなかった内容を英語でどう表現するか調べ、クラスメイトと共有しましょう。

Gather Information

Listening プレゼンテーションの音声を聞いてキーワードを書き取りましょう。

DL 25　CD2-04 ～ CD2-08

Installing solar panels

Facts

_____

_____

_____

Advantages	**Disadvantages**

Reading　次の英文を読んで、内容を理解しましょう。後の設問にも答えましょう。

🎧 DL 25　💿 CD2-04 ～ 💿 CD2-08

Should homeowners install solar panels?

1　Clean energy like solar energy has been attracting people's attention around the world. For example, you may have seen mega solar farms in the countryside. These are made by big corporations. However, these days, individuals can use solar panels to turn their private homes into power stations. Do you think it is beneficial for homeowners to
5　install solar panels?

2　In 2021, the International Energy Agency set a global goal to promote renewable energy sources. They announced that by 2030 global solar power generation needs to be four times greater than it was in 2020. The Japanese government also released its plan to make a law that requires installation of solar panels on newly built houses. The
10　Tokyo metropolitan government followed the plan and made it a regulation. However, the plan received a mixed response and further discussion is needed before it can be put into practice nationwide.

3　Now, let's look at some advantages of having solar panels on our houses. Most importantly, we can save money on electricity bills. In some cases, we can even sell the
15　surplus electricity to the power companies. In addition, we can realize self-sufficiency in power generation. It is crucial that people in Japan prepare for blackouts caused by disasters. While the power is out, electricity generated by solar panels can provide us with power for lights and communication tools.

4　In contrast, some people think there are more disadvantages to installing solar
20　panels on private homes. For instance, it is often pointed out that solar panels can be costly. Even with financial support from the government, the cost for installation of solar panels may be a financial burden for some households. Besides, there is the problem
25　of reliability. Because the weather heavily influences the output from solar panels, it is challenging to stop relying on the current power supply system completely.

68

5 As you can see, people have various opinions about installing solar panels.
30 Homeowners should consider the cost, reliability, and contribution to the environment
when they decide whether solar panels are beneficial to them. (338 words)

✐Notes   the International Energy Agency「国際エネルギー機関」 self-sufficiency「自給自足」

🔍 Focus on Meaning

本文の内容と一致するものはT、一致しないものはFを選びましょう。

1. Mega solar farms are mainly built by the government. T | F

2. Tokyo has not made a regulation relating to solar panel installation. T | F

3. Solar panels can reduce the cost of electricity. T | F

4. Solar panels can prevent natural disasters. T | F

5. Solar energy production is not affected by weather conditions. T | F

🔍 Focus on Vocabulary

本文に登場する1〜5の語の同義語▤または反意語⬌として最も適切な語を選びましょう。

1. beneficial [ℓ.4] ⬌ useful   official   harmful   bare

2. install [ℓ.5] ⬌ integrate   remove   discount   spare

3. renewable [ℓ.6] ▤ disposable   profitable   wasteful   sustainable

4. surplus [ℓ.15] ⬌ flat   extra   lacking   cheap

5. reliability [ℓ.25] ▤ security   instability   flexibility   crisis

🔍 Focus on Grammar   〈It 〜 to ...〉構文・〈It 〜 that ...〉構文

主語が長くなるときに、意味を持たない形式上の主語itを文頭に置き、文末にto不定詞やthat節を用いて主語となる内容を後で言うことができます。

例 **It** is beneficial for homeowners **to** install solar panels.
　 It is crucial **that** people in Japan prepare for blackouts.

📖✎ Task   第4段落のitを形式上の主語にした文に下線を引き、意味を確認しましょう。

Role Play Discussion

Situation を読み、3人一組となっ
てそれぞれの役割に分かれディス
カッションをしましょう。メモは
キーワードレベルで準備し、右ペー
ジの表現例も参考にしながら、細
部は考えながら話しましょう。

Situation
市長が、個人宅のソーラーパネル設置を義
務付ける条例案を出すべきか考えています。
タウンミーティングで住民Aは賛成の意見、住民
Bは反対の意見を述べようとしています。住民の
意見を聞き、市長は条例案を出すかどうかを決定
しましょう。

Memo

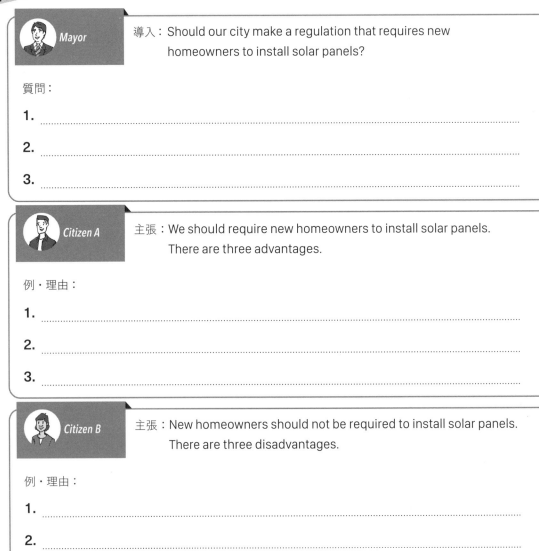

Mayor

導入：Should our city make a regulation that requires new homeowners to install solar panels?

質問：

1. ....

2. ....

3. ....

Citizen A

主張：We should require new homeowners to install solar panels. There are three advantages.

例・理由：

1. ....

2. ....

3. ....

Citizen B

主張：New homeowners should not be required to install solar panels. There are three disadvantages.

例・理由：

1. ....

2. ....

3. ....

- What do you think about ...?
- Is it necessary for the city to ...?
- Could you tell me in detail?
- Can you think of an example?

- First, by requiring solar panels, the city can ...
- If I were you, I would ...
- It is ideal that new homeowners ...
- In summary, it is more beneficial to ...

- Installing solar panels causes problems such as ...
- Do you have any thoughts on ...?
- Many homeowners may suffer from ...
- I believe it is crucial that ...

住民の話をもとに、市長は最終的な決断を下しましょう。住民Aと住民Bの発言内容を簡単に振り返りながら、決断の理由を明確に示しましょう。

	Mayor's Decision
結論	I decided (to / not to) make a regulation that requires new homeowners to install solar panels because A/B gave me a good reason.
まとめ・理由	・A/B said that _____. ・The citizens will highly appreciate the opinion. ・A/B's idea of (_____) is good, but _____.

Review Your Role Play を振り返って、自分がどのように話したかをチェックしましょう。

Q1 相手に話すきっかけを与えたり、情報を求めたりするときの表現を使いましたか。

　　□ 何度か使った　　□ 1回使った　　□ 使わなかった

Q2 Cue Expressionsやそれと同等の機能を持つ表現を使いましたか。

　　□ 何度か使った　　□ 1回使った　　□ 使わなかった

Q3 メッセージを伝えるときに、〈It ~ to ...〉構文や〈It ~ that ...〉構文を使ってみましたか。

　　□ 何度か使った　　□ 1回使った　　□ 使わなかった

Q4 自分の主張に対して、理由を明確に述べることができましたか。

　　□ 複数の理由を述べた　　□ 1つの理由を述べた　　□ 理由を述べられなかった

Write Your Opinion

この章で学んだ語句を3つ以上使って、次のテーマについて100語以上のパラグラフを書きましょう。

⇨ 解答欄は p. 137

Theme If you were the mayor, would you require new homeowners to install solar panels?

Further Activities

この章で学んだ内容に関連する情報を追加で調べ、クラスメイトとシェアしましょう。

Example 太陽光の他に日本で導入が進んでいる再生可能エネルギーには、どのようなものがあるでしょうか。

Unit 9

Should Japan ban the sale of pets?

日本はペットの売買を禁止すべきか?

多くの人が犬や猫などのペットとの暮らしを楽しんでいます。一方、ペットの売買を禁止する国もあります。どのような背景や意見があるのでしょうか。

Listen and Interact

 Sophia の意見に対する友達の意見を聞き、表にチェックを入れましょう。

Sophia's opinion: Japan should ban the sale of pets.

 DL 26   CD2-09

	Yota	Tim	Mina	Ray
Agrees	☐	☐	☐	☐
Disagrees	☐	☐	☐	☐

 A. 次の表現の意味を確認し、音声に続いて声に出してみましょう。

B. 再度 *1st* Round の音声を聞き、使われている次の表現に○をつけましょう。

🎧 DL 27   ◉ CD2-10

Formulaic Expressions *Interrupting Politely / Buying Time to Think*

📍 会話の途中で議論に加わるとき

Could I say something?   Hold on a moment.   May I interrupt you?

So sorry to interrupt you, but ...   Can I just add something here?

📍 時間を稼ぐとき

Let me see.   Well, let me think about it.   How can I explain ...?

That's a difficult question to answer, but ...   I can't answer that right away.

73

3rd Round 1st Roundの音声を聞いて下線部を埋めましょう。下線部は1語とは限りません。

Sophia: In France, the sale of cats and dogs at pet shops will be ¹_____ in 2024. I think Japan should also ban the sale of pets. What do you think, Yota?

Yota: ²_____ your idea, Sophia. I see so many puppies and kittens sold in pet shops. I like animals, but I don't want to imagine ³_____ to them when nobody buys them. Also ...

Tim: ⁴_____, Yota?

Yota: Sure, Tim.

Tim: I understand your feeling, but pet shops are necessary to ⁵_____ suitable pets. ⁶_____ pet shops, consumers can get healthy pets at reasonable prices. They also provide pet owners lots of advice on ⁷_____ pets. What do you think, Mina?

Mina: Well, let me think about it .... All right. I think pet shops should not sell animals. Cats, dogs, fish, hamsters, reptiles, ... all of them ⁸_____ human beings. They have the right to live happily. In my view, buying and selling animals by humans is not ⁹_____. How about you, Ray?

Ray: Well, I think pet shops can help people find the perfect pet, so pet shops ¹⁰_____.

⌒Focus on **Sounds**

1st Roundの音声を利用して、音読とシャドーイングを行いましょう。内容を理解しながら発音ポイントにも注意し、表に沿って5点満点で自己評価しましょう。

発音ポイント▶ [æ] [ei] [e] Japan should also ban the sale of pets. [ℓ.2]

音読 テキストを見ながら音読		内容・発音を意識して読めた度合い 5 4 3 2 1
パラレル音読 テキストを見ながら音声と同時に音読		内容・発音を意識して言えた度合い 5 4 3 2 1
シャドーイング テキストを見ないで音声の直後に復唱		ついていけた度合い 5 4 3 2 1

1〜5の文を読み、ペット売買の禁止に賛成派(a)か反対派(b)かを判断しましょう。

1. Many breeders will go out of business.   a | b
2. Pet shops do not treat animals humanely.   a | b
3. Some breeders keep too many dogs in bad conditions.   a | b
4. Pet shop owners can give beneficial advice to customers.   a | b
5. Pet shops make it easy to find animals that people want to own as pets.   a | b

Interaction これまでの内容を参考にして、下線部に語句を補いながら対話をしましょう。

A: I'm wondering if Japan should ban the sale of pets. What do you think?

B: **That's a difficult question to answer, but** I think _____.

A: Why do you think so?

B: Because ...

→ うまく言えなかった内容を英語でどう表現するか調べ、クラスメイトと共有しましょう。

Gather Information

Listening プレゼンテーションの音声を聞いてキーワードを書き取りましょう。

🎧 DL 28　◉ CD2-11 〜 ◉ CD2-15

Banning the sale of pets

Facts

_____

_____

_____

Advantages   Disadvantages

_____   _____

_____   _____

_____   _____

_____   _____

Should Japan ban the sale of pets?

1　Pets are big business in the world, and pet shops have been booming. In France, however, it is said that about 100,000 pets are abandoned annually by their owners, breeders, or shops. To solve the issue, France has decided to ban the sale of cats and dogs in pet shops beginning in 2024. Many pets are abandoned in Japan as well. Some
5　people believe Japan should take a similar action against pet sales.

2　The pet market is growing every year. It is estimated to be as large as 1.7 trillion yen, so the industry makes up a big share of Japan's economy. The sales amount includes actual pets, pet food, pet commodities, grooming, medical care, and insurance. However, as many as 23,800 cats and dogs were reportedly euthanized in shelters in
10　2020. Although the number has become smaller compared to past years, many animals continue to be killed every year.

3　Under the circumstances, there are two advantages of banning the sale of pets. First, the lives of thousands of animals will be saved. Those who want to have a pet need to find one through adoption from either an animal conservation group or their
15　acquaintances. This time-consuming process might bother the prospective owners but helps them become more responsible for having a pet. Second, the ban follows bioethics. To abide by the ethics that all lives should be treated equally, stricter rules are necessary to protect animal rights and animal welfare.

4　However, some people are against the banning of pet sales. First, pet shops and
20　breeders claim that they will go out of business. Following the ban, pets might not be as popular as they are now. Accordingly, the size of the pet industry will shrink because the consumption of pet-related goods and services will decrease. On top of
25　that, pet lovers will have difficulty finding a new pet. With no new pets to choose from, people will not be emotionally fulfilled. In short, humans' well-being is at stake.

[5] Although banning pet sales may sound drastic, breeders, pet stores, and consumers
30 would at least start thinking deeply about animal rights. If humans valued animal
welfare more, pets could live happier lives. In return, humans would become happier,
too.

(369 words)

✍*Notes*   euthanize「～を安楽死させる」   shelter「保護施設」   bioethics「生命倫理」

Focus on **Meaning**

本文の内容と一致するものはT、一致しないものはFを選びましょう。

1. Japan has decided to ban the sale of cats and dogs.   T｜F
2. It was reported in 2020 that about 23,800 cats and dogs were born in Japan.   T｜F
3. The adopting process might make owners more responsible for having a pet.   T｜F
4. The banning of pet sales may cause the pet market to shrink.   T｜F
5. People will be happier if they take good care of their pets.   T｜F

Focus on **Vocabulary**

本文に登場する1～5の語の同義語📒または反意語⬌として最も適切な語を選びましょう。

1. estimate   [ℓ.6]   📒   calculate   believe   establish   neglect
2. commodity   [ℓ.8]   📒   advantage   treasure   credit   goods
3. acquaintance [ℓ.15]   ⬌   aquarium   novelty   stranger   friend
4. prospective   [ℓ.15]   ⬌   future   uninterested   incorrect   potential
5. welfare   [ℓ.18]   📒   worry   appeal   well-being   self-defense

Focus on **Grammar**   比較

ものごとの量や度合いを説明するために比較級を使うと、情報が相手に伝わりやすくなります。また、〈as+形容詞+as〉のような原級比較を用いて、直後の数値を強調することもできます。

例 The pet market is estimated to be **as large as** 1.7 trillion yen.
The number has become **smaller** compared to past years.
This helps them become **more responsible** for having a pet.

📝 Task 第4段落にある比較表現に下線を引き、意味を確認しましょう。

Role Play Discussion

Situation を読み、3人一組となっ
てそれぞれの役割に分かれディス
カッションをしましょう。メモは
キーワードレベルで準備し、右ペー
ジの表現例も参考にしながら、細
部は考えながら話しましょう。

Situation 環境大臣（Minister of the Environment）
がペットの殺処分を減らすためにペット
売買を禁止するべきか考えています。動物保
護団体の代表（A）は禁止に賛成、ペットショップ
協会の代表（B）は禁止に反対を訴えています。各
代表の意見を聞き、環境大臣はペット売買の禁止
に踏み切るかどうかを決定しましょう。

Memo

Minister of the Environment

導入： I wonder if Japan should ban the sale of pets. Please let me hear
your opinions.

質問：

1. ....

2. ....

3. ....

Leader of Animal Conservation Group (A)

主張： I think Japan should ban the sale of pets totally. Let me explain
why we should do so.

例・理由：

1. ....

2. ....

3. ....

Head of Pet Store Association (B)

主張： I don't think we should ban the sale of pets. Let me tell you why.

例・理由：

1. ....

2. ....

3. ....

Agenda:
1. ~~~~
2. ~~~~
3. Discussion: Should Japan ban the sale of pets?
4. ~~~~

■ As the Minister of the Environment, I wonder if ...
■ What is good / bad about ...?
■ So sorry to interrupt you, but ...
■ I would appreciate your input.

■ Minister, you absolutely need to ...
■ Banning the sale of pets has some advantages. First, ...
■ In my experience, I have seen ...
■ Can I just add something here?

■ Could I say something?
■ Minister, you should not ...
■ Pet shops contribute to society by ...
■ Our customers say ... is better than ...

Decision Making

各代表の話をもとに、環境大臣は最終的な決断を下しましょう。動物保護団体の代表Aとペットショップ協会の代表Bの発言内容を簡単に振り返りながら、決断の理由を明確に示しましょう。

	Minister's Decision
結論	I decided (to / not to) ban the sale of pets because A/B gave me a good reason.
まとめ・理由	・A/B said that _____ . ・I understood the points he/she mentioned. ・A/B's idea of (　　　　　　) is good, but _____ .

Review Your Role Play

Role Play を振り返って、自分がどのように話したかをチェックしましょう。

Q1 会話の途中で議論に加わったり、時間を稼いだりするときの表現を使うことができましたか。
　　☐ 何度か使った　　☐ 1回使った　　☐ 使わなかった

Q2 Cue Expressionsやそれと同等の機能を持つ表現を使いましたか。
　　☐ 何度か使った　　☐ 1回使った　　☐ 使わなかった

Q3 メッセージを伝えるときに、いろいろな比較表現を使うことができましたか。
　　☐ 何度か使った　　☐ 1回使った　　☐ 使わなかった

Q4 自分の主張に対して、理由を明確に述べることができましたか。
　　☐ 複数の理由を述べた　　☐ 1つの理由を述べた　　☐ 理由を述べられなかった

Write Your Opinion

この章で学んだ語句を3つ以上使って、次のテーマについて100語以上のパラグラフを書きましょう。
⇨解答欄は p. 138

Theme　If you were the Minister of the Environment, would you ban the sale of pets?

Further Activities

この章で学んだ内容に関連する情報を追加で調べ、クラスメイトとシェアしましょう。

Example　国内外におけるペット売買の現状やペットに関する規制について、調べてみましょう。

Unit 10

Should Japan introduce a four-day workweek?

日本は労働日数を週4日にすべきか？

ワーク・ライフ・バランスの重要性から労働時間の短縮が話題になっています。週の労働日数を4日に減らすことは、日本社会にどのような影響をもたらすでしょうか。

Listen and Interact

 1st Round　Tim の意見に対する友達の意見を聞き、表にチェックを入れましょう。

Tim's opinion: Japan should introduce a four-day workweek.

 DL 29　 CD2-16

	Sophia	Yota	Emma	Ray
Agrees	☐	☐	☐	☐
Disagrees	☐	☐	☐	☐

 2nd Round　**A.** 次の表現の意味を確認し、音声に続いて声に出してみましょう。
B. 再度 *1st Round* の音声を聞き、使われている次の表現に○をつけましょう。

 DL 30　 CD2-17

> **Formulaic Expressions**　*Correcting Misunderstanding*
>
> 📍 誤解を解くとき
> That's not what I mean.　　You must have misunderstood me.
> Let me clarify.　　What I really meant was ...
>
> 📍 論点を戻すとき
> That's not the problem.　　Come to the point.　　What we are discussing is ...
> That's an important point, but let's get back to ...
> ... has nothing to do with my argument.

3rd Round 1st Roundの音声を聞いて下線部を埋めましょう。下線部は 1 語とは限りません。

Tim: I heard some companies reduced weekly working days from ¹ _____ _____ in Ireland. I think Japan should also introduce a four-day workweek.

Sophia: Tim, ² _____, you said you don't care how much you work if you get a good salary, didn't you?

Tim: That's not what I mean. ³ _____ that if workers work hard, they can produce the same output in four days as they do in five. What do you think, Sophia?

Sophia: I agree that ⁴ _____ is important, but working five days seems just right to me. It will give workers a ⁵ _____ _____. What's your opinion, Yota?

Yota: I agree with Tim. My parents are both working. ⁶ _____ day off, they could spend more time at home. Emma, what do you think?

Emma: I think workers need at least five days ⁷ _____. You can spend time with your parents on two-day weekends, Yota.

Yota: ⁸ _____. I think good ideas often come out of doing various things outside the office. Do you agree, Ray?

Ray: Well, ⁹ _____, if people have more free time, they can go on trips or do their hobbies. Sightseeing spots and facilities for sports and culture will have more visitors. That will ¹⁰ _____ the local economy.

♪ Focus on Sounds

1st Roundの音声を利用して、音読とシャドーイングを行いましょう。内容を理解しながら発音ポイントにも注意し、表に沿って 5 点満点で自己評価しましょう。

発音ポイント ● [w] [r] Some companies <u>r</u>educed <u>w</u>eekly <u>w</u>orking days. [ℓ.1]
　　　　　　　　 ※唇の動かし方は類似している一方、舌の動きが異なることに注意

音読 テキストを見ながら 音読		内容・発音を意識して読めた度合い 5　　4　　3　　2　　1
パラレル音読 テキストを見ながら 音声と同時に音読		内容・発音を意識して言えた度合い 5　　4　　3　　2　　1
シャドーイング テキストを見ないで 音声の直後に復唱		ついていけた度合い 5　　4　　3　　2　　1

82

Idea Generation 1〜5の文を読み、週4日労働制に賛成派(a)か反対派(b)かを判断しましょう。

1. Working for five days a week is reasonable.   a | b
2. Young workers can gain experience by working more days.   a | b
3. More time for recreation is necessary to perform well at work.   a | b
4. Some companies are worried about lower levels of productivity.   a | b
5. Long working weeks do not guarantee a worker's good performance.   a | b

Interaction これまでの内容を参考にして、下線部に語句を補いながら対話をしましょう。

A: Should Japan introduce a four-day workweek?

B: I think / don't think so because _____.

A: So you mean _____?

B: Yes, exactly. / No, **that's not what I mean**. **Let me clarify**. ...

→ うまく言えなかった内容を英語でどう表現するか調べ、クラスメイトと共有しましょう。

Gather Information

Listening プレゼンテーションの音声を聞いてキーワードを書き取りましょう。

DL 31　CD2-18 〜 CD2-22

Introducing a four-day workweek

Facts

Advantages

Concerns

Reading 次の英文を読んで、内容を理解しましょう。後の設問にも答えましょう。

🎧 DL 31　⦿ CD2-18 ~ ⦿ CD2-22

Should Japan introduce a four-day workweek?

1 Shortening the working week is one way to realize a better work-life balance. Companies in some countries have started letting their employees work for four days instead of five. There are pros and cons to introducing a four-day workweek system.

2 According to a Japanese government survey, male full-time workers worked 47.9
5 hours per week on average in 2000, which means they worked almost six days a week. In the past, working overtime was seen as a virtue in Japan, but people have realized that it causes low productivity. Furthermore, large-scale experiments conducted by an Irish firm showed favorable results in cutting working days from five to four. The firm predicted this trend may become more common in the near future.

10 3 Supporters of a four-day workweek claim that there are two advantages. First, a four-day workweek will improve workers' well-being. They can feel refreshed, for example, by playing sports for more days. They will be healthier in the long run, which would reduce health care costs. Also, more time spent with family and friends will make people happier, which might lead to a better working atmosphere. In addition, fewer
15 working days will bring better work performance overall. Not only will workers have more opportunities to rest, but they will also be able to improve their professional skills and knowledge. As a result, their creativity and productivity may improve.

4 A four-day workweek has some risks as well. First, some employers are concerned about productivity. If the same workload cannot be done in a shorter amount of time,
20 they must employ more workers, which may cost more in the end. Next, many people doubt that employers will pay workers the same salary after reducing the days they work. If their salary is cut, workers may have to find an additional job. Moreover, companies with a
25 four-day workweek may lower their competitiveness against their rivals. Thus, the number of working days has to be changed all at once throughout the country, which may
30 require a long debate.

5 Some people do not mind working as they do for five days a week, while others want fewer working days to prioritize their private lives. It will take some time for society to reach a consensus about this issue.

(372 words)

⌕Focus on *Meaning*

本文の内容と一致するものは T、一致しないものは F を選びましょう。

1. People in Japan currently think of long working weeks as a virtue.   T | F
2. The four-day workweek is said to improve the creativity of workers.   T | F
3. Having fewer working days will cause more companies to lose their employees. T | F
4. Shortening the working week may force some workers to find other jobs.   T | F
5. Introducing a shorter workweek needs further discussion among citizens.   T | F

⌕Focus on *Vocabulary*

本文に登場する 1 ～ 5 の語の同義語 ➖ または反意語 ⬌ として最も適切な語を選びましょう。

1. virtue   [ℓ.6]   ➖   evil   vice   main   merit
2. favorable   [ℓ.8]   ➖   kind   undesirable   unfortunate   positive
3. refreshed [ℓ.11]   ⬌   relaxed   revitalized   excited   exhausted
4. private   [ℓ.32]   ⬌   public   personal   restricted   remote
5. consensus [ℓ.33]   ⬌   agreement accord   opposition   consent

⌕Focus on *Grammar*　　関係代名詞の非制限用法

先行詞と関係代名詞 which の間にカンマ (,) を添えることで、前述の内容に補足的に説明を加えることができます。名詞以外にも、前述の句や節全体が先行詞になる場合があります。関係代名詞 that にはこの用法はありません。

例 Male full-time workers worked 47.9 hours per week on average in 2000, **which** means they worked almost six days a week.

The number of working days has to be changed all at once throughout the country, **which** may require a long debate.

✎ Task 第 3 段落の関係代名詞の非制限用法を含む文に下線を引き、意味を確認しましょう。

Role Play Discussion

Situation を読み、3 人一組となっ
てそれぞれの役割に分かれディス
カッションをしましょう。メモは
キーワードレベルで準備し、右ペー
ジの表現例も参考にしながら、細
部は考えながら話しましょう。

Situation

　　ある会社の CEO がフルタイム社員の勤務
を 4 日制にするべきか悩んでいます。役員 A
は短縮に賛成、役員 B は反対の立場を取っていま
す。役員の意見を聞き、CEO は勤務日数の短縮を
導入するかどうかを決定しましょう。

Memo

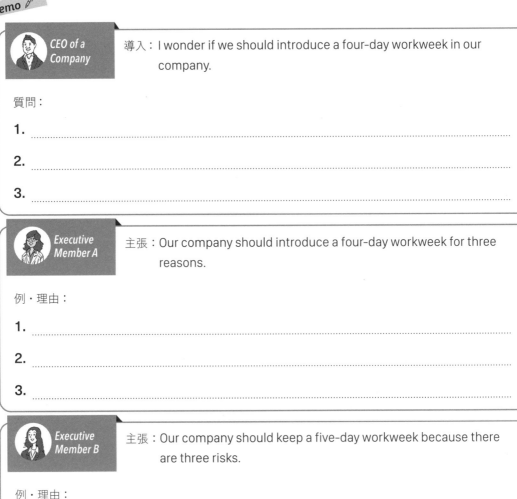

CEO of a Company

導入：I wonder if we should introduce a four-day workweek in our company.

質問：

1. ....

2. ....

3. ....

Executive Member A

主張：Our company should introduce a four-day workweek for three reasons.

例・理由：

1. ....

2. ....

3. ....

Executive Member B

主張：Our company should keep a five-day workweek because there are three risks.

例・理由：

1. ....

2. ....

3. ....

■ What are the pros and cons of a four-day workweek?

■ Will our company ...?

■ That's an important point, but let's get back to ...

■ What we are discussing is ...

■ We should end a five-day workweek, which ...

■ The four-day workweek is beneficial because ...

■ Our employees can ...

■ You may say ..., but that's not the problem.

■ We should not introduce a four-day workweek, which ...

■ Some of the employees said to me that ...

■ A four-day workweek may not work well because ...

■ What I really meant was ...

２人の役員の話をもとに、CEOは最終的な決断を下しましょう。役員Aと役員Bの発言内容を簡単に振り返りながら、決断の理由を明確に示しましょう。

	CEO's Decision
結論	I decided (to / not to) introduce a four-day workweek because A/B gave me a good reason.
まとめ・理由	・A/B said that _____ . ・This point sounds very important. ・A/B's idea of (_____) is good, but _____ .

 Role Playを振り返って、自分がどのように話したかをチェックしましょう。

Q1 相手の誤解を解いたり、論点を戻したりするときの表現を使いましたか。
☐ 何度か使った ☐ 1回使った ☐ 使わなかった

Q2 Cue Expressionsやそれと同等の機能を持つ表現を使いましたか。
☐ 何度か使った ☐ 1回使った ☐ 使わなかった

Q3 メッセージを伝えるときに、関係代名詞の非制限用法を使ってみましたか。
☐ 何度か使った ☐ 1回使った ☐ 使わなかった

Q4 自分の主張に対して、理由を明確に述べることができましたか。
☐ 複数の理由を述べた ☐ 1つの理由を述べた ☐ 理由を述べられなかった

Write Your Opinion

この章で学んだ語句を３つ以上使って、次のテーマについて100語以上のパラグラフを書きましょう。

⇨解答欄は p. 139

Theme If you were the CEO, would you introduce a four-day workweek?

Further Activities

この章で学んだ内容に関連する情報を追加で調べ、クラスメイトとシェアしましょう。

Example 世界の国や地域の平均労働時間や、ワーク・ライフ・バランスを実現する働き方の例について、調べてみましょう。

Unit 11

Should children's video game time be limited by law?

子どものゲーム時間を
法規制すべきか？

18歳未満の人にゲーム時間の規制を行っ
ている自治体があります。法律や条例で
ゲーム時間を制限することの是非につい
て考えてみましょう。

Listen and Interact

Mina の意見に対する友達の意見を聞き、表にチェックを入れましょう。

Mina's opinion: Children's video game time should be limited by law.

 DL 32    CD2-23

	Ray	Emma	Yota	Sophia
Agrees	☐	☐	☐	☐
Disagrees	☐	☐	☐	☐

A. 次の表現の意味を確認し、音声に続いて声に出してみましょう。

B. 再度 *1st* Round の音声を聞き、使われている次の表現に○をつけましょう。

 DL 33    CD2-24

Formulaic Expressions ⟩ *Stating Something as a Fact*

● 見聞きした情報を客観的に伝えるとき

According to an article I read, ...   These days, many people ...

Scientists have recently discovered ...

● 情報を一般化して述べるとき

As everyone knows, ...   It is generally accepted that ...

There is no doubt that ...   Nobody will deny that ...

Mina: According to an article I read, a prefecture in Japan has a regulation that limits the amount of time people under 18 can play video games. I think children's game time should be limited by law. What do you think, Ray?

Ray: That sounds ¹_____ to me. Children can control their game time if they are guided ²_____ by adults, so I don't think we need such a law. Instead, we should give some ³_____ to parents. Emma, what's your opinion?

Emma: ⁴_____ watching a display too long causes physical problems such as eye fatigue and ⁵_____. However, I think this regulation is not effective. The amount of ⁶_____ internet use, not just game time, should be controlled. Yota, do you agree with my opinion?

Yota: Well, I believe that a separate law for game time is necessary. ⁷_____ _____, some games don't require an internet connection. Children tend to play such games endlessly. The law helps people ⁸_____ _____ their game time. What do you think, Sophia?

Sophia: ⁹_____ children have the right to play video games, but that doesn't mean they can play for hours and hours. To enjoy video games ¹⁰_____, children need strict laws to guide them.

ⅭFocus on Sounds

1st Roundの音声を利用して、音読とシャドーイングを行いましょう。内容を理解しながら発音ポイントにも注意し、表に沿って5点満点で自己評価しましょう。

発音ポイント ▶ [l] [r] A prefecture in Japan has a regulation that limits ... [ℓ.1]

音読 テキストを見ながら音読		内容・発音を意識して読めた度合い
		5　4　3　2　1
パラレル音読 テキストを見ながら音声と同時に音読		内容・発音を意識して言えた度合い
		5　4　3　2　1
シャドーイング テキストを見ないで音声の直後に復唱		ついていけた度合い
		5　4　3　2　1

1〜5の文を読み、ゲーム時間の規制に賛成派(a)か反対派(b)かを判断しましょう。

1. Limiting game time is not effective.　　　　　　　　　　　　　a | b
2. People under 18 can control their game time on their own.　　　a | b
3. Playing video games for too long is bad for children's health.　　a | b
4. Parents can discuss and decide the gaming time with their children.　a | b
5. There should be a legal limit on how long children can play video games.　a | b

Interaction これまでの内容を参考にして、下線部に語句を補いながら対話をしましょう。

A: Do you think children's video game time should be limited by law?

B: I think so / don't think so because _____.

A: Can you tell me more about your opinion?

B: **These days, many people** ...

→ うまく言えなかった内容を英語でどう表現するか調べ、クラスメイトと共有しましょう。

Gather Information

Listening プレゼンテーションの音声を聞いてキーワードを書き取りましょう。

DL 34　CD2-25 〜 CD2-29

Limiting children's video game time by law

Facts

Advantages	Disadvantages

Reading 次の英文を読んで、内容を理解しましょう。後の設問にも答えましょう。

🎧 DL 34 💿 CD2-25 ~ 💿 CD2-29

Should children's video game time be limited by law?

1 These days, many children have game consoles in their homes. With easy access to the Internet, children spend a lot of time playing video games. In a survey conducted by an internet provider, about 30% of primary school students play video games for more than two hours a day. Furthermore, 16% play more than three hours.

5 2 Dealing with this issue, Kagawa prefecture, for example, created an ordinance that limits children's video game time but does not include any form of punishment. Specifically, children are allowed to play video games for 60 minutes each day on weekdays, and 90 minutes per day on weekends and holidays. After the ordinance was enacted, the prefecture reported that the number of children using screens for more

10 than three hours a day was reduced by about five percent between 2017 and 2020.

3 One advantage of having the law is that it creates a positive chain reaction in society. First, people in society pay more attention to children's lives. Checking how long they spend playing video games and using the Internet, organizations such as schools and local governments can help children control their screen time. Second,

15 families will have more chances to discuss the issue of screen time. Talking with their parents, children can learn the appropriate limits. As a consequence, society can protect children from getting addicted to games and the Internet.

4 On the other hand, some are against the law. First, they claim that the law violates people's rights to make their own decisions. According to them, game time management

20 should not be regulated by law. Instead, families should give children opportunities to learn how to use their time effectively on their own. Second, although there is no punishment for breaking the law, this could change in the future. If a form of punishment were added to the law, it could create a negative social bias against video

25 games and internet use.

5 There is no doubt that game time should be controlled. The problem is who controls it

and to what degree—the law or families. Society needs to carefully consider the positive

30 and negative effects of making such a law and the rights of children.   (363 words)

Focus on **Meaning**

本文の内容と一致するものはT、一致しないものはFを選びましょう。

1. About 30% of primary school students play video games on weekends.   T | F
2. Kagawa's ordinance limits children's time for video games to one hour on
   weekdays.   T | F
3. Children in Kagawa will be punished if they play games too much.   T | F
4. The law makes families think about children's screen time.   T | F
5. Some claim that families should help children manage their own time.   T | F

Focus on **Vocabulary**

本文に登場する1～5の語の同義語■または反意語⬌として最も適切な語を選びましょう。

1. ordinance   [ℓ.5]   ■   chaos   law   riot   disorder
2. enact   [ℓ.9]   ■   encode   estimate   fasten   legislate
3. appropriate   [ℓ.16]   ■   accurate   irregular   unsuitable   proper
4. consequence   [ℓ.16]   ⬌   result   cause   effect   end
5. regulate   [ℓ.20]   ⬌   monitor   adjust   neglect   control

Focus on **Grammar**   分詞構文

付帯状況、時、条件、理由、譲歩などの意味を表す従属節を主節に加えるとき、主節と主語が同じ場合は主語を省略して動詞を分詞(～ing/～ed)にして表せます。省略する主語は主節と同じことが原則ですが、異なる場合もあります(独立分詞構文)。

例 <u>Dealing with this issue</u>, <u>Kagawa prefecture</u> created an ordinance. [分詞構文]
　　　分詞　　　　　　　　　従属節・主節共通の主語

<u>All things considered</u>, <u>children</u> should not play games too much. [独立分詞構文]
　従属節の主語+分詞　　　主節の主語

Task 第3段落の分詞構文に下線を引き、意味を確認しましょう。

Role Play Discussion

Situation を読み、3人一組となっ
てそれぞれの役割に分かれディス
カッションをしましょう。メモは
キーワードレベルで準備し、右ペー
ジの表現例も参考にしながら、細
部は考えながら話しましょう。

Situation

市長が子どもたちの教育を考えてゲーム
時間の規制をするべきか悩んでいます。住民
A は規制に賛成、住民 B は規制に反対の意見を
持っています。住民の意見を聞き、市長はゲーム
時間を規制するかどうかを決定しましょう。

Memo

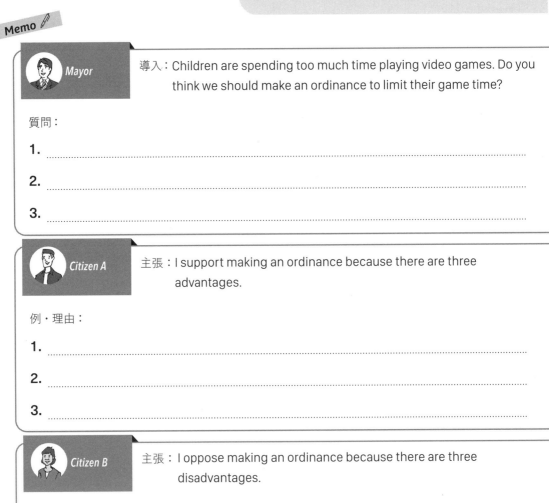

Mayor

導入：Children are spending too much time playing video games. Do you
think we should make an ordinance to limit their game time?

質問：

1. ....

2. ....

3. ....

Citizen A

主張：I support making an ordinance because there are three
advantages.

例・理由：

1. ....

2. ....

3. ....

Citizen B

主張：I oppose making an ordinance because there are three
disadvantages.

例・理由：

1. ....

2. ....

3. ....

- Games are very popular because ...
- As everyone knows, children ...
- It is generally accepted that ...
- Does anyone want to ...?

- These days, many children ...
- Playing video games too much is ...
- The proposed ordinance will ...
- Frankly speaking, I ...

- Children had better ...
- First of all, making such a law will ...
- Generally speaking, ...
- Scientists have recently discovered ...

２人の住民の話をもとに、市長は最終的な決断を下しましょう。住民Ａと住民Ｂの発言内容を簡単に振り返りながら、決断の理由を明確に示しましょう。

	Mayor's Decision
結論	I decided (to / not to) make an ordinance that limits children's video game time because A/B gave me a good reason.
まとめ・理由	・A/B said that _____ . ・The opinion was very persuasive to me. ・A/B's idea of ( ) is good, but _____ .

 Role Play を振り返って、自分がどのように話したかをチェックしましょう。

Q1 情報を客観的に伝えたり、一般化して述べたりするときの表現を使いましたか。

　　☐ 何度か使った　　☐ 1回使った　　☐ 使わなかった

Q2 Cue Expressionsやそれと同等の機能を持つ表現を使いましたか。

　　☐ 何度か使った　　☐ 1回使った　　☐ 使わなかった

Q3 メッセージを伝えるときに、分詞構文を使うことができましたか。

　　☐ 何度か使った　　☐ 1回使った　　☐ 使わなかった

Q4 自分の主張に対して、理由を明確に述べることができましたか。

　　☐ 複数の理由を述べた　　☐ 1つの理由を述べた　　☐ 理由を述べられなかった

Write Your Opinion

この章で学んだ語句を３つ以上使って、次のテーマについて100語以上のパラグラフを書きましょう。
⇨解答欄は p. 140

 Theme If you were the mayor, would you make an ordinance that limits children's video game time?

Further Activities

この章で学んだ内容に関連する情報を追加で調べ、クラスメイトとシェアしましょう。

Example 世界における子どものゲーム時間規制について、調べてみましょう。

Unit 12

Should cashless payment be promoted further in Japan?

キャッシュレス決済は日本で
さらに促進されるべきか？

近年、キャッシュレス決済がますます一般
化してきています。私たちの生活において、
現金が不要となる日も近いのでしょうか。

Listen and *Interact*

1st Round

Ray の意見に対する友達の意見を聞き、表にチェックを入れましょう。

Ray's opinion: Cashless payment should be promoted further in Japan.

 DL 35    CD2-30

	Mina	Tim	Emma	Yota
Agrees	☐	☐	☐	☐
Disagrees	☐	☐	☐	☐

2nd Round

A. 次の表現の意味を確認し、音声に続いて声に出してみましょう。

B. 再度 *1st Round* の音声を聞き、使われている次の表現に○をつけましょう。

 DL 36    CD2-31

Formulaic Expressions ▸ *Expressing Contrasting Points of View*

📍 論点を対比するとき

While ..., ...   Some .... Others ...   In contrast (to ...), ...
Contrary to ..., ...   On (the) one hand, ... On the other hand, ...

📍 論点を比較するとき

Compared to ..., ...   As well as ..., ...   Like ..., ...   Similarly, ...
Unlike ..., ..., which is different from / similar to ...

Ray: These days, cashless payment is getting very popular. For example, I often use my train IC card to ¹ _____. It's very convenient, so I think cashless payment should be promoted further in Japan. What do you think, Mina?

Mina: Well, ² _____, cashless payment is convenient because people don't need to carry notes or coins. On the other hand, people ³ _____ _____ may not be able to buy things. I personally prefer paying in cash and hope cashless payment ⁴ _____ much. What about you, Tim?

Tim: I agree with you, Mina. I ⁵ _____ when I use my credit card. I often can't remember how much I spent. The same thing ⁶ _____ _____ smartphone payment services. When I show a bar code from a payment app, I don't feel I spent money. It's too simple. Emma?

Emma: Some feel ⁷ _____ risky like you, Tim, but others claim that it's helpful. You see, I never know how much money I'll need. That's why I pay with my smartphone. What do you think, Yota?

Yota: ⁸ _____ people who prefer cash, I feel cashless payment should be promoted further in Japan. It is becoming ⁹ _____, but Japan is slow to adopt it. With more and more ¹⁰ _____ to Japan, we must become a cashless-friendly country.

🔍 Focus on Sounds

*1st Round*の音声を利用して、音読とシャドーイングを行いましょう。内容を理解しながら発音ポイントにも注意し、表に沿って５点満点で自己評価しましょう。

発音ポイント ❶ [ʃ] [s]   Ca**sh**le**ss** payment **sh**ould be promoted further in Japan. [ℓ.3]

音読 テキストを見ながら音読		内容・発音を意識して読めた度合い				
		5	4	3	2	1
パラレル音読 テキストを見ながら音声と同時に音読		内容・発音を意識して言えた度合い				
		5	4	3	2	1
シャドーイング テキストを見ないで音声の直後に復唱		ついていけた度合い				
		5	4	3	2	1

Idea Generation 1〜5の文を読み、キャッシュレスの推進派(a)か反対派(b)かを判断しましょう。

1. You may only need a smartphone to go shopping.   a | b
2. Cash is bulky and takes up much space in your wallet.   a | b
3. You do not have to touch any cash to pay for something.   a | b
4. When your smartphone is broken, you cannot pay for anything.   a | b
5. Paying in cash helps you avoid spending more money than necessary.   a | b

Interaction これまでの内容を参考にして、下線部に語句を補いながら対話をしましょう。

A: Which do you prefer, cash or cashless payment?

B: **While** I understand the advantages of _____ , I think _____ is better.

A: Can you tell me more about your opinion?

B: Well, _____ is convenient because _____ . ....

⤳ うまく言えなかった内容を英語でどう表現するか調べ、クラスメイトと共有しましょう。

Gather Information

Listening プレゼンテーションの音声を聞いてキーワードを書き取りましょう。

🎧 DL 37 ◉ CD2-32 ～ ◉ CD2-36

Cashless payment

Facts

Disadvantages | **Advantages**

Should cashless payment be promoted further in Japan?

|1| Many people in the world shop without cash. Cashless payments have become common in Japan, too. There is a report that as of 2021, 32.5% of shopping was done with credit cards, IC cards, or smartphone payment services. However, some other countries have more actively adopted cashless payment systems. Thus, there is an opinion that
5 Japan could promote cashless payment further.

|2| Japan is often referred to as a cash society. Even though the government has tried to increase the use of cashless payments to 40% of purchases, many privately-owned shops still accept only cash. In contrast, in other countries such as South Korea, Canada, and many EU countries, the rate of purchases made using cashless payment is consistently
10 over 50%. In Sweden, cash in circulation was only 1.7% of its GDP in 2015. There, 60% of bank branches do not deal with cash any more. As cashless payment systems have become common, the banks have been able to reduce the cost of dealing with cash such as maintaining ATMs.

|3| However, there are arguments against promoting a cashless society. First of
15 all, cashless payments are a bother to some. Those without mobile phones will face difficulties in a cashless society. Second, people can feel how much they have earned and spent when using cash. Third, cash is more reliable in emergency situations. Cashless payments cannot be relied on in blackouts, internet outages, or when a smartphone breaks.

20 |4| Nevertheless, it is important to note the fact that promoting cashless payment systems will bring some benefits to society. First, cashless payments save time when shopping. People do not have to search their pockets for notes or coins. Second, fewer crimes may
25 happen. Because there is no tangible money to steal, cases of theft may decrease. Finally, currency exchange may be unnecessary. While traveling internationally, the time and cost of
30 exchanging money can be saved.

5 Promoting a cashless society seems to have some advantages. In contrast, we should note the fact that cashless payments are inconvenient for some people. Some think that cashless payment improves society; others think that cash is easy to handle and robust in emergencies. Each has its advantages, but the world is heading toward cashless payment systems. Do you think Japan should follow the trend? (375 words)

Focus on **Meaning**

本文の内容と一致するものは T、一致しないものは F を選びましょう。

1. Approximately 30% of shopping in Japan was done in cash in 2021. T | F
2. About 60% of Swedish people shop using a cashless payment method. T | F
3. Some people may have a hard time living in a cashless society. T | F
4. We can depend more on cash in emergency situations. T | F
5. Using a credit card costs more than paying in cash when traveling abroad. T | F

Focus on **Vocabulary**

本文に登場する 1 〜 5 の語の同義語 🟰 または反意語 ⇔ として最も適切な語を選びましょう。

1. circulation [ℓ.10] 🟰 ambition   block   circuit   distribution
2. bother [ℓ.15] 🟰 delight   comfort   trouble   noise
3. tangible [ℓ.25] ⇔ actual   concrete   obvious   untouchable
4. currency [ℓ.27] 🟰 stream   cash   rush   flow
5. robust [ℓ.33] ⇔ unstable   fit   powerful   artificial

Focus on **Grammar**   同格の that

ある情報や事実、人の考えなどについて文を添えて説明したいとき、同格の接続詞 that を使い、その後に説明文を示します。この場合の that 節では関係代名詞節とは異なり、完全な文(節)を使います。

例 There is <u>an opinion</u> **that** <u>Japan could promote cashless payment further</u>.

It is important to note <u>the fact</u> **that** <u>promoting cashless payment systems will bring some benefits to society</u>.

Task 第 5 段落の同格の that を含む文に下線を引き、意味を確認しましょう。

Role Play Discussion

Situation を読み、3人一組となってそれぞれの役割に分かれディスカッションをしましょう。メモはキーワードレベルで準備し、右ページの表現例も参考にしながら、細部は考えながら話しましょう。

Situation

市長が、街の経済を活性化するためにキャッシュレス決済を促進するべきか悩んでいます。副市長(A)は賛成、市長室長(B)は反対の立場から進言しています。副市長と市長室長の意見を聞き、市長はキャッシュレス決済を促進するかどうかを決定しましょう。

| Mayor | 導入：I want citizens to enjoy shopping and stimulate the local economy. Should cashless payment be promoted further in our city? |

質問：

1. ....

2. ....

3. ....

| Deputy Mayor (A) | 主張：I think we should promote cashless payment further in our city. Here are some reasons. |

例・理由：

1. ....

2. ....

3. ....

| Secretary (B) | 主張：I don't think we should promote cashless payment further in our city. I have some reasons. |

例・理由：

1. ....

2. ....

3. ....

Please tell me your opinion.

Do you think cashless payment is ...?

Some people .... Others ...

Compared to cash / cashless payment, ...

The good points of cashless payment are ...

Unlike cash payment, cashless payment ...

While some might give an opinion that cash is ...

Promoting cashless payment will benefit the city because ...

Cash payment has advantages, ...

People without devices for cashless payment cannot ...

Contrary to the popular belief that ...

Cash is ..., which is different from / similar to ...

２人の話をもとに、市長は最終的な決断を下しましょう。副市長Ａと市長室長Ｂの発言内容を簡単に振り返りながら、決断の理由を明確に示しましょう。

	Mayor's Decision
結論	I decided (to / not to) promote cashless payment further because A/B gave a good reason.
まとめ・理由	・A/B said that _____. ・I was convinced by the opinion. ・A/B's idea of (　　　　　　) is good, but _____.

 Role Play を振り返って、自分がどのように話したかをチェックしましょう。

Q1 論点を対比・比較するときの表現を使いましたか。
　　□何度か使った　　□1回使った　　□使わなかった

Q2 Cue Expressionsやそれと同等の機能を持つ表現を使いましたか。
　　□何度か使った　　□1回使った　　□使わなかった

Q3 メッセージを伝えるときに、同格のthatを使ってみましたか。
　　□何度か使った　　□1回使った　　□使わなかった

Q4 自分の主張に対して、理由を明確に述べることができましたか。
　　□複数の理由を述べた　　□1つの理由を述べた　　□理由を述べられなかった

Write Your Opinion

この章で学んだ語句を３つ以上使って、次のテーマについて100語以上のパラグラフを書きましょう。　　　　　　　　　　　　　　　　　　　　　　　　⇨解答欄は p. 141

Theme If you were the mayor, would you promote cashless payment further in your city?

Further Activities

この章で学んだ内容に関連する情報を追加で調べ、クラスメイトとシェアしましょう。

Example 海外のキャッシュレス決済の状況について、具体的に調べてみましょう。

Unit 13

Should social media companies censor their platforms?

ソーシャルメディア会社は
投稿内容を検閲すべきか？

ソーシャルメディアは、人がさまざまな意見を述べることができる場です。しかし、好ましくない投稿が社会問題となっている中、それらを防ぐために投稿内容は検閲されるべきでしょうか。

Listen and Interact

1st Round

Emma の意見に対する友達の意見を聞き、表にチェックを入れましょう。

Emma's opinion: Social media companies should censor their platforms.

 DL 38   CD2-37

	Tim	Yota	Mina	Sophia
Agrees	☐	☐	☐	☐
Disagrees	☐	☐	☐	☐

2nd Round

A. 次の表現の意味を確認し、音声に続いて声に出してみましょう。

B. 再度 *1st Round* の音声を聞き、使われている次の表現に○をつけましょう。

 DL 39   CD2-38

Formulaic Expressions   *Making a Counterargument*

● 丁寧に反論するとき

I'm not sure if ...   I wonder if you realize that ...   That's not always true.

Are you aware that ...?   I'm sorry I have to say this, but ...

● 強く反論するとき

I'm not convinced.   I can't quite understand why ...

You said that ..., but ...   That doesn't make sense to me.

I have a completely different opinion on that.

3rd Round 1stRoundの音声を聞いて下線部を埋めましょう。下線部は1語とは限りません。

Emma: I received an email from the school. It warned that students should be careful about ¹＿＿＿＿＿＿＿＿＿＿＿＿＿＿ on social media. I think social media companies should censor their platforms. What do you think, Tim?

Tim: I agree with you, Emma. Harmful content should be removed from social media. Many people are ²＿＿＿＿＿＿＿＿＿＿ online posts that express hate towards certain groups of people. Also, cyberbullying on social media ³＿＿＿＿＿＿＿＿＿＿＿ among young people. What would you say, Yota?

Yota: I'm not convinced. In Japan, ⁴＿＿＿＿＿＿＿＿＿＿＿＿＿＿＿＿ is guaranteed by the constitution. If social media companies censor and remove some content based on ⁵＿＿＿＿＿＿＿＿＿＿＿＿, it is a violation of the constitution. Don't you agree, Mina?

Mina: ⁶＿＿＿＿＿＿＿＿＿ censorship violates any laws. The content should be censored somehow, though. If influential people such as politicians post ⁷＿＿＿＿＿＿＿＿＿＿＿＿, some people can be brainwashed. ⁸＿＿＿＿＿＿＿＿＿ on social media is also a serious problem. To protect users, the companies should take responsibility for censorship. What do you think, Sophia?

Sophia: Well, ⁹＿＿＿＿＿＿＿＿＿＿＿＿＿＿ checking posts costs companies a huge amount of money. It would hurt the companies financially. I think there is still something we can do ¹⁰＿＿＿＿＿＿＿＿＿ censoring the content.

♪Focus on Sounds

1stRoundの音声を利用して、音読とシャドーイングを行いましょう。内容を理解しながら発音ポイントにも注意し、表に沿って5点満点で自己評価しましょう。

発音ポイント ▶ [ou] [ʌ] S̲o̲cial media c̲o̲mpanies should censor their platforms. [ℓ.2~3]

音読		内容・発音を意識して読めた度合い
テキストを見ながら音読		5　　4　　3　　2　　1
パラレル音読		内容・発音を意識して言えた度合い
テキストを見ながら音声と同時に音読		5　　4　　3　　2　　1
シャドーイング		ついていけた度合い
テキストを見ないで音声の直後に復唱		5　　4　　3　　2　　1

Idea Generation 1〜5の文を読み、ソーシャルメディア会社による検閲に賛成派(a)か反対派(b)かを判断しましょう。

1. People have a right to express anything freely.   a | b
2. Monitoring user information can lead to data leaks.   a | b
3. Censorship prevents careless comments on social media.   a | b
4. Censorship by social media companies can reduce cybercrime.   a | b
5. The cost of censorship can be a financial burden to social media companies.   a | b

Interaction これまでの内容を参考にして、下線部に語句を補いながら対話をしましょう。

A: Should social media companies censor their platforms?

B: I think so / don't think so because _____.

A: **I can't quite understand why** _____.

B: Well, let me explain in detail. ...

→ うまく言えなかった内容を英語でどう表現するか調べ、クラスメイトと共有しましょう。

Gather Information

Listening プレゼンテーションの音声を聞いてキーワードを書き取りましょう。

🎧 DL 40   💿 CD2-39 ~ 💿 CD2-43

Censoring social media platforms

Facts

....

....

....

Advantages	Disadvantages

次の英文を読んで、内容を理解しましょう。後の設問にも答えましょう。

DL 40　CD2-39 ～ CD2-43

Should social media companies censor their platforms?

1　Social media has a lot of potential to enhance our communication. Social media platforms provide people certain advantages such as reaching a large audience, networking, and promoting products. However, some of the content on social media is harmful and hurts people's feelings. Recently, there has been a debate about whether
5　social media companies should censor their platforms or not.

2　In 2022, over 4.5 billion people in the world used social media. Accordingly, social media influences people's lives in both good and bad ways. Unfortunately, online harassment has been increasing worldwide. The National Police Agency in Japan reported that annually about 2,000 teenagers had become victims of cybercrime. Under
10　these circumstances, the necessity of social media censorship has been debated.

3　There are several advantages to censorship. First, it can remove insensitive and threatening posts, which can protect people from online harassment. It can also help parents protect their children from exposure to inappropriate content. Second, it can reduce cybercrime, such as fraud and identity theft. For instance, internet scams often
15　use social media to target their victims. Third, it can protect people from misleading information such as fake news. By monitoring the platforms, social media companies can help people judge whether the news is trustworthy or not.

4　Censorship, however, has some drawbacks. Firstly, it may violate the freedom of expression. Individuals would lose their opportunities to express their viewpoints if
20　social media companies could delete posts according to their own rules. Secondly, censorship can be misused for political purposes or for the manipulation of information. As a result, social media companies may play a powerful role in controlling society. Finally,
25　users' private information may be in danger. Storing a huge amount of personal data collected for censorship, the companies may leak or sell the collected data to third parties.

30　⑤ Social media platforms are powerful communication tools, and they should not be misused. Censorship is one of the options to eliminate harmful posts, but it also has a possibility to overly control the general public. Can we keep counting on users' morals, or should we count on censorship?

(346 words)

✍ *Note*　the National Police Agency「警察庁」

⌒Focus on **Meaning**

本文の内容と一致するものはT、一致しないものはFを選びましょう。

1. Social media affects people's lives in both good and bad ways.　　　T｜F
2. About 2,000 elderly people become victims of cybercrime every year.　　　T｜F
3. Censorship can protect children from harmful content.　　　T｜F
4. Social media companies can create their own rules for censorship.　　　T｜F
5. Social media companies have little risk of leaking personal information.　　　T｜F

⌒Focus on **Vocabulary**

本文に登場する1～5の語の同義語■または反意語■として最も適切な語を選びましょう。

1. harmful　　　[ℓ.4]　⬌　bad　　risky　　harassing　　favorable
2. insensitive　　　[ℓ.11]　⬌　considerate　　heartless　　responsible　　active
3. scam　　　[ℓ.14]　■　law　　fraud　　punishment　　crime
4. trustworthy　　　[ℓ.17]　■　practical　　reliable　　skeptical　　valuable
5. manipulation　　　[ℓ.21]　■　manual　　control　　negotiation　　expression

⌒Focus on **Grammar**　　過去形と過去完了形

過去の一時点で起こった事実などを表すときは過去形を使います。過去の一時点までに動作や状態が継続あるいは完了したことを表すときは過去完了形を使います。時間軸を点でとらえるのが過去形、線でとらえるのが過去完了形です。

例　Mary **began** living in Paris in 2016.
　　She **had lived** in Paris for seven years by the time she moved to London.

Task　第2段落の過去形・過去完了形を含む文に下線を引き、意味を確認しましょう。

Role Play Discussion

Situation を読み、3人一組となっ
てそれぞれの役割に分かれディス
カッションをしましょう。メモは
キーワードレベルで準備し、右ペー
ジの表現例も参考にしながら、細
部は考えながら話しましょう。

Situation

ソーシャルメディア会社のCEOが投稿内
容の検閲を行うべきかを会議の議題に挙げ
ています。営業部長(A)は検閲に賛成、法律顧問
(B)は反対の立場を取っています。会社関係者の
意見を聞き、CEOは検閲を行うかどうかを決定し
ましょう。

CEO of a Social Media Company

導入：I wonder if we should begin censoring our social media platform. What is your idea?

質問：

1. ....

2. ....

3. ....

Sales Manager (A)

主張：We should censor our platform. There are three reasons.

例・理由：

1. ....

2. ....

3. ....

Legal Advisor (B)

主張：We should not censor our platform. There are three risks.

例・理由：

1. ....

2. ....

3. ....

■ Please tell me some advantages /
disadvantages of ...
■ Can you tell me some examples?
■ Are you aware that ... on our platform?
■ You said that ..., but ...

■ Regarding the situation of social media, ...
■ One of the advantages of censorship is ...
■ I wonder if you realize that social media ...
■ Our users once told us ...

■ I can't quite understand why ...
■ I have a completely different opinion on ...
■ One drawback of censorship is ...
■ Before the days of the Internet, ...

Decision Making

2人の会社関係者の話をもとに、CEOは最終的な決断を下しましょう。営業部長Aと法律顧問Bの発言内容を簡単に振り返りながら、決断の理由を明確に示しましょう。

	CEO's Decision
結論	I decided (to / not to) censor our platform because A/B gave me a good reason.
まとめ・理由	・A/B said that ＿＿＿＿＿＿＿＿＿＿＿＿＿＿＿＿＿＿＿＿＿ . ・This opinion sounds beneficial to our company. ・A/B's idea of (　　　　　　) is good, but ＿＿＿＿＿＿＿＿＿ .

Review Your Role Play

Role Playを振り返って、自分がどのように話したかをチェックしましょう。

Q1 相手の意見に反論するときの表現を使うことができましたか。

　□何度か使った　　□1回使った　　□使わなかった

Q2 Cue Expressionsやそれと同等の機能を持つ表現を使いましたか。

　□何度か使った　　□1回使った　　□使わなかった

Q3 メッセージを伝えるときに、過去形・過去完了形を意識して使うことができましたか。

　□何度か使った　　□1回使った　　□使わなかった

Q4 自分の主張に対して、理由を明確に述べることができましたか。

　□複数の理由を述べた　　□1つの理由を述べた　　□理由を述べられなかった

Write Your Opinion

この章で学んだ語句を3つ以上使って、次のテーマについて100語以上のパラグラフを書きましょう。

⇨解答欄は p. 142

Theme　If you were the CEO, would you censor your social media platform?

Further Activities

この章で学んだ内容に関連する情報を追加で調べ、クラスメイトとシェアしましょう。

Example　さまざまなソーシャルメディアにおける検閲の状況について、調べてみましょう。

Unit 14

Should Japan invest more in space development?

日本はさらに宇宙開発に
投資すべきか？

世界の中には宇宙開発に多額の投資を
行っている国があります。日本も追随し
て、開発のためにさらに税金を投入する
べきでしょうか。

Listen and *Interact*

1st *Round*

Yota の意見に対する友達の意見を聞き、表にチェックを入れましょう。

Yota's opinion: Japan should invest more in space development.

🎧 DL 41　　◎ CD2-44

	Emma	Ray	Mina	Tim
Agrees	☐	☐	☐	☐
Disagrees	☐	☐	☐	☐

2nd *Round*

A. 次の表現の意味を確認し、音声に続いて声に出してみましょう。

B. 再度 *1st* Round の音声を聞き、使われている次の表現に○をつけましょう。

🎧 DL 42　　◎ CD2-45

Formulaic Expressions ⟩ *Speculating / Hypothesizing*

🔵 推論するとき

Apparently, ...　　Probably, ...　　Supposedly, ...　　Presumably, ...

It seems like ...　　Judging from ..., ...　　It is highly likely that ...

I guess / suppose / assume / infer (that) ...　　I could possibly argue that ...

🔵 仮定するとき

Provided that ...　　If I were to ..., ...　　I would ...

It is assumed that ...　　Hypothetically speaking, ...

3rd Round 1st Roundの音声を聞いて下線部を埋めましょう。下線部は１語とは限りません。

Yota: The other day, I saw some news about commercial space trips. Apparently, private citizens flew from the US into space and ¹ _____

_____. I believe Japan should invest more in space development. What do you think, Emma?

Emma: I ² _____ you, Yota. Going to space has become big business in the world. In addition, for more advanced data networks, we need more sophisticated ³ _____. Also, we need to develop better ⁴ _____ them.

Yota: ⁵ _____. What's your opinion, Ray?

Ray: Well, I guess the story is not that simple. I don't think Japan should invest so much in it. There are a lot of problems to solve here ⁶ _____, such as global warming. What would you say, Mina?

Mina: I'm hopeful that space exploration will result in new discoveries. ⁷ _____ _____ Japan can keep contributing its technologies and human resources to space development, such as maintaining the space station and exploring beyond ⁸ _____. How about you, Tim?

Tim: I am worried about economic disparity in the world, which influences the capability to ⁹ _____ in space development. Only rich countries will find benefits from space, and poor countries ¹⁰ _____.

✐*Note* economic disparity「経済格差」

Focus on Sounds

1st Roundの音声を利用して、音読とシャドーイングを行いましょう。内容を理解しながら発音ポイントにも注意し、表に沿って５点満点で自己評価しましょう。

発音ポイント❷ [ə] I saw some news about commercial space trips. [ℓ.1]

音読 テキストを見ながら 音読		内容・発音を意識して読めた度合い				
		5	4	3	2	1
パラレル音読 テキストを見ながら 音声と同時に音読		内容・発音を意識して言えた度合い				
		5	4	3	2	1
シャドーイング テキストを見ないで 音声の直後に復唱		ついていけた度合い				
		5	4	3	2	1

Idea Generation 1～5の文を読み、宇宙開発に賛成派（a）か反対派（b）かを判断しましょう。

1. We may discover new scientific knowledge. a | b
2. You might be able to live on another planet. a | b
3. New satellites make the Internet much faster. a | b
4. Poor countries have fewer chances to participate in space projects. a | b
5. Launching rockets requires a lot of energy, which is not eco-friendly. a | b

Interaction これまでの内容を参考にして、下線部に語句を補いながら対話をしましょう。

A: Should Japan invest more in space development?

B: I think so. / I don't think so.

A: Why do you think so? / Why not?

B: **Apparently**, space development is / isn't beneficial for humans because _____.

うまく言えなかった内容を英語でどう表現するか調べ、クラスメイトと共有しましょう。

Gather Information

Listening プレゼンテーションの音声を聞いてキーワードを書き取りましょう。

DL 43 CD2-46 ~ CD2-50

Investing in space development

Facts

Advantages	Disadvantages

Reading 次の英文を読んで、内容を理解しましょう。後の設問にも答えましょう。

🎧 DL 43 ⊙ CD2-46 ~ ⊙ CD2-50

Should Japan invest more in space development?

1 Today, some countries in the world are making a lot of investments in space development. Japan is one of them. The term "space development" covers all activities to launch devices and humans into space in order to improve human life as well as to satisfy humans' explorative spirit.

5 2 Japan is a big investor in space development and supports the development of space technologies. Since the US, China, Russia, and India have spent more on space development, the Japanese government has increased the amount of its investment budget to over 500 billion yen in 2022. Why are these countries so keen on developing space?

10 3 Space development has at least three advantages. First, further developments in scientific technologies and knowledge can be expected. Presumably, the results of such development will bring about the next generation technologies of IoT and 6G, which will improve people's lives. Second, space development requires large projects that will lead to more job opportunities. For example, the creation of new satellites involves the

15 collaboration of many companies and researchers. Third, if another habitable planet were found, many global issues such as food shortages and overpopulation could be solved.

4 Meanwhile, some disadvantages of space development have been pointed out. The primary concern is the huge cost. Research projects on space require a large amount

20 of money mostly coming from taxes. The money could be spent directly on solving many issues on the earth. The next concern is space debris. It is assumed that there are 22,000 pieces of debris floating in the earth's orbit. By launching rockets and satellites, more debris will be produced.

25 Additionally, it will be difficult to create a safe living environment in space. Humans are not designed to withstand the high levels of radioactivity or the lack of gravity in space. The burden on the human body

30 would be significant if people began to live in space.

5 In conclusion, space development has many potential benefits for human beings. The benefits should be shared equally across nations, not only enjoyed by the countries that invested in them. Since space development is costly, people have to consider whether the benefits are truly worth the money.

(358 words)

35

✐*Notes* space debris「宇宙ゴミ」 radioactivity「放射能」

♪*Focus on* Meaning

本文の内容と一致するものはT、一致しないものはFを選びましょう。

1. The purpose of space development is to better humans' lives. **T | F**
2. Japan has decided to decrease the budget for space development in 2022. **T | F**
3. Space development will create more jobs. **T | F**
4. Food shortages could be solved if humans found another habitable planet. **T | F**
5. If Japan joined a space project, space debris would be decreased. **T | F**

♪*Focus on* Vocabulary

本文に登場する1〜5の語の同義語🟰または反意語🔁として最も適切な語を選びましょう。

1. satisfy   [ℓ.4]   🔁   disappoint   criticize   control   convince
2. budget   [ℓ.8]   🔁   expenditure   saving   account   credit
3. collaboration [ℓ.15] 🟰   separation   teamwork   division   hostility
4. habitable   [ℓ.15] 🔁   livable   cozy   barren   tragic
5. potential   [ℓ.32] 🟰   unlikely   inherent   imaginable   possible

♪*Focus on* Grammar   仮定法過去と仮定法過去完了

起こりうる可能性が低い現在のことや架空の想定を述べるとき、If節の動詞を過去形にします（通例be動詞の時はwere）。主節にはwould, could, mightなど過去形の助動詞を用います。過去のことがらの場合はIf節の動詞を過去完了形に、主節の助動詞の後を完了形にします。

例 **If** you **had** one trillion yen, what **would** you buy?
    If I **had worked** harder, I **might have become** a general manager.

Task 第3段落と第4段落で、それぞれ1文ずつ仮定法を含む文に下線を引き、意味を確認しましょう。

Role Play Discussion

Situation を読み、3人一組となっ
てそれぞれの役割に分かれディス
カッションをしましょう。メモは
キーワードレベルで準備し、右ペー
ジの表現例も参考にしながら、細
部は考えながら話しましょう。

Situation

文部科学大臣(Minister of MEXT)は宇宙
開発の予算を増やすべきか悩んでいます。
官僚Aは予算を増やして宇宙開発を推進するべき、
官僚Bは予算を削減し他の用途に使うべきだと考
えています。官僚たちの意見を聞き、文部科学大
臣は予算の方針を決定しましょう。

Memo ✏

✍ *Note*　　MEXT = Ministry of Education, Culture, Sports, Science and Technology

---

Minister of MEXT

導入：I have been wondering whether the ministry should increase the budget for space development. Do you think Japan should invest more in space development?

質問：

1. ....

2. ....

3. ....

Government Officer A

主張：I think Japan should invest more in space development. There are three advantages.

例・理由：

1. ....

2. ....

3. ....

Government Officer B

主張：I think Japan should not invest more in space development. I'll tell you the reasons.

例・理由：

1. ....

2. ....

3. ....

- Do you think space development is ...?
- Could you tell me the reasons why you think so?
- If humans discovered a new planet to live on, would they ...?
- Without the promotion of space development, would Japan ...?

- We should increase the budget because Japan ...
- First, space development is .... For example, ...
- Second, if humans were to live in space, ...
- Hypothetically speaking, Japan would be able to ... with space technology.

- We should not increase the budget because ...
- First, space development could ... if ...
- Judging from the current situation, ...
- It is highly likely that promoting space development will ...

2人の官僚たちの話をもとに、文部科学大臣は最終的な決断を下しましょう。官僚Aと官僚Bの発言内容を簡単に振り返りながら、決断の理由を明確に示しましょう。

	Minister's Decision
結論	I decided (to / not to) invest more in space development because A/B gave me a good reason.
まとめ・理由	・A/B said that _____. ・The opinion was very persuasive to me. ・A/B's idea of ( ) is good, but _____.

Role Playを振り返って、自分がどのように話したかをチェックしましょう。

Q1 推論や仮定をするときの表現を使いましたか。
　　 ☐何度か使った 　　☐1回使った 　　☐使わなかった

Q2 Cue Expressionsやそれと同等の機能を持つ表現を使いましたか。
　　 ☐何度か使った 　　☐1回使った 　　☐使わなかった

Q3 メッセージを伝えるときに、仮定法を使ってみましたか。
　　 ☐何度か使った 　　☐1回使った 　　☐使わなかった

Q4 自分の主張に対して、理由を明確に述べることができましたか。
　　 ☐複数の理由を述べた 　　☐1つの理由を述べた 　　☐理由を述べられなかった

Write Your Opinion

この章で学んだ語句を3つ以上使って、次のテーマについて100語以上のパラグラフを書きましょう。　　　　　　　　　　　　　　　　　　　　　　　　⇨解答欄は p. 143

Theme If you were the Minister of MEXT, would you invest more in space development?

Further Activities

この章で学んだ内容に関連する情報を追加で調べ、クラスメイトとシェアしましょう。

Example 日本や世界における、政府による宇宙開発予算や技術支援について、調べてみましょう。

 Formulaic Expressions in Focus : *Drawing Conclusions / Summing Up*

Unit 15

Should public baths and hot springs accept people with tattoos?

日本の公衆浴場・温泉地は タトゥーを受け入れるべきか?

近年、海外からの観光客の増加に伴い、公衆浴場や温泉地でのタトゥー客受け入れの是非が議論されています。タトゥー客の入浴は全面的に許容されるべきでしょうか。

Listen and *Interact*

 1st *Round*

Sophia の意見に対する友達の意見を聞き、表にチェックを入れましょう。

Sophia's opinion: Public baths and hot springs should accept people with tattoos.

🎧 DL 44   💿 CD2-51

	Yota	Emma	Mina	Ray
Agrees	☐	☐	☐	☐
Disagrees	☐	☐	☐	☐

 2nd *Round*

A. 次の表現の意味を確認し、音声に続いて声に出してみましょう。
B. 再度 *1st* Round の音声を聞き、使われている次の表現に○をつけましょう。

🎧 DL 45   💿 CD2-52

Formulaic Expressions ▸ *Drawing Conclusions / Summing Up*

📍 結論を述べるときの表現

In conclusion, ...   Most importantly, ...   All things considered, ...
My final thought is ...

📍 これまでの発言や論点をまとめるときの表現

To sum up, ...   Summing up, ...   Let me recap ...
As you can see, ...   Let me give you my main points again.

Sophia: I love hot springs, but I don't like it when my friends can't join me because of their tattoos. Public baths and hot springs in Japan should accept people with tattoos. What do you think, Yota?

Yota: To be honest, ¹_____ when seeing people who have full-body tattoos. You know, in Japan, tattoos have been ²_____ _____ antisocial behaviors. I heard some people get tattooed to scare people. ³_____, it's better to keep the current practice. Emma, what's your opinion?

Emma: I understand your opinion, but at public baths, there are more important rules than ⁴_____ people with tattoos.

Yota: Such as ...?

Emma: ⁵_____ away from bathwater. ⁶_____ _____ my point. Having tattoos shouldn't be treated in the same way as other important rules. Mina, what do you think?

Mina: I completely agree with you. I know there's ⁷_____ behind tattoos in Japan, but some people now see tattoos as a form of fashion. There's ⁸_____ when taking a bath with those people, right, Ray?

Ray: Well, I don't think ⁹_____ will accept people with tattoos even if the bathhouses do. Like Yota, many people including myself still instinctively ¹⁰_____ of people with tattoos.

🔍 Focus on Sounds

1st Roundの音声を利用して、音読とシャドーイングを行いましょう。内容を理解しながら発音ポイントにも注意し、表に沿って5点満点で自己評価しましょう。

| 発音ポイント ➤ [u] [u:] | Public baths ... sh**ou**ld accept people with tatt**oo**s. [ℓ.2~3] |

音読		内容・発音を意識して読めた度合い				
テキストを見ながら音読		5	4	3	2	1
パラレル音読		内容・発音を意識して言えた度合い				
テキストを見ながら音声と同時に音読		5	4	3	2	1
シャドーイング		ついていけた度合い				
テキストを見ないで音声の直後に復唱		5	4	3	2	1

1. People with tattoos tend to be seen as gangsters.   a | b
2. Hotels and public baths can attract more guests.   a | b
3. Tattoos have become a way to express one's fashion.   a | b
4. Anyone should have the right to experience Japanese culture.   a | b
5. Some people feel uncomfortable when seeing people with tattoos.   a | b

Interaction これまでの内容を参考にして、下線部に語句を補いながら対話をしましょう。

A: Should public baths and hot springs accept people with tattoos?

B: I think so / don't think so because _____.

A: I see. Are there any other reasons?

B: Well, I believe _____. **As you can see**, ...

→ うまく言えなかった内容を英語でどう表現するか調べ、クラスメイトと共有しましょう。

Gather Information

Listening プレゼンテーションの音声を聞いてキーワードを書き取りましょう。

🎧 DL 46 ◉ CD2-53 ~ ◉ CD2-57

Accepting people with tattoos

Facts

Against	**For**

次の英文を読んで、内容を理解しましょう。後の設問にも答えましょう。

DL 46 CD2-53 ~ CD2-57

Should public baths and hot springs accept people with tattoos?

1 Hot springs are important tourist attractions in Japan. No matter which prefecture you visit, you will see many tourists enjoying them. As the country welcomes more tourists from abroad who want to experience and enjoy Japanese culture, one unavoidable issue is whether public baths should accept tattooed people.

2 Let's see how popular hot springs are. In 2019, the Japan Tourism Agency asked foreign tourists to participate in a survey. The results showed that going to a hot spring was the fifth most popular activity on the tourists' wish lists. As for tattoos, a study in the United States revealed that more Americans had tattoos in 2019 compared to 2012. This suggests that tattoos are becoming popular and that more tourists with tattoos may come to Japan.

3 However, bathhouses could lose some domestic customers by letting tattooed people come in. The biggest reason is Japan's long history with tattoos. For centuries, tattoos in Japan have been associated with antisocial behaviors. They are largely known as a symbol of organized criminal groups. Also, they used to be a type of punishment for criminals back in the Edo period. Since these negative impressions have been ingrained in the society, many Japanese people feel scared or uncomfortable being naked around people with tattoos.

4 That being said, there are some benefits of accepting people with tattoos at public baths. First, it may give people opportunities to change their views of tattoos. Lately, an increasing number of people get tattooed simply to be fashionable. If people get more chances to see tattoos used in a fashionable way, it may help them recognize tattoos differently. In addition, it may become a chance for the public to learn about diversity. Some groups of people get tattooed for religious or cultural reasons. For those people, tattoos are part of their identity. By accepting

tattooed people, bathhouses can be a place to gain intercultural understanding, which
30 is a step toward ending discrimination.

⑤ Most importantly, this issue will not be solved overnight. No matter how hard it can
be, we need to actively discuss it and find a reasonable solution.   (348 words)

✎Note   the Japan Tourism Agency「観光庁」

Focus on Meaning

本文の内容と一致するものはT、一致しないものはFを選びましょう。

1. Fifty percent of foreign tourists wanted to go to hot springs in 2019.   T | F
2. The number of Japanese people with tattoos has been increasing.   T | F
3. In Japan, tattoos are associated with criminal organizations.   T | F
4. Some people feel uncomfortable being naked in bathhouses.   T | F
5. People get tattooed for various reasons.   T | F

Focus on Vocabulary

本文に登場する1〜5の語の同義語 ＝ または反意語 ⇔ として最も適切な語を選びましょう。

1. unavoidable   [ℓ.4]   ⇔   necessary   debatable   optional   essential
2. ingrain   [ℓ.15]   ＝   crop   initiate   occupy   implant
3. diversity   [ℓ.26]   ⇔   dissimilarity   heterogeneity   variance   uniformity
4. discrimination [ℓ.30]   ⇔   equity   prejudice   injustice   hatred
5. overnight   [ℓ.31]   ＝   lazily   swiftly   gradually   sleeplessly

Focus on Grammar   〈no matter ＋ 疑問詞〉

発表や議論の場では、〈no matter ＋ 疑問詞（how, what, which, whoなど）〉の表現を
使うことで、主張や論点を強調することができます。

例 **No matter which** prefecture you visit, you will see many tourists.
No matter what others say, I believe your story.

Task   第5段落の〈no matter ＋ 疑問詞〉を含む文に下線を引き、意味を確認しましょう。

Role Play Discussion

Situation を読み、3人一組となってそれぞれの役割に分かれディスカッションをしましょう。メモはキーワードレベルで準備し、右ページの表現例も参考にしながら、細部は考えながら話しましょう。

Situation

温泉経営者協会の会長が、規則の改定を考えています。タトゥーがある人の入浴について、経営者Aは入浴受け入れ、経営者Bは入浴拒否の立場を取っています。経営者の意見を聞き、会長は規則を改定するかどうかを決定しましょう。

Memo

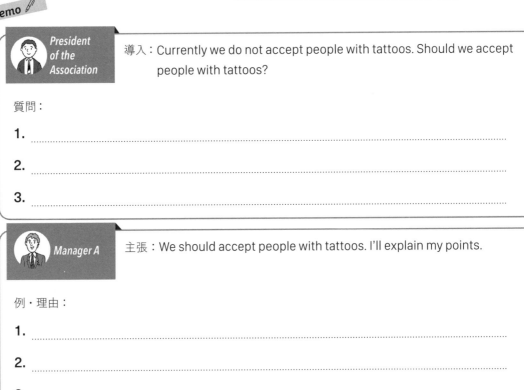

President of the Association

導入：Currently we do not accept people with tattoos. Should we accept people with tattoos?

質問：

1. ....

2. ....

3. ....

Manager A

主張：We should accept people with tattoos. I'll explain my points.

例・理由：

1. ....

2. ....

3. ....

Manager B

主張：We should not accept people with tattoos. Let me explain in detail.

例・理由：

1. ....

2. ....

3. ....

No Tattoos

Tattoos

- Could you give some pros and cons of changing the rule?
- Do many of your customers ...?
- Do you have any trouble at your facility?
- How would the change affect ...?

- First of all, our bathhouses .... For example, ...
- No matter how / when / who ...
- Let me give you my main points again.
- My final thought is ...

- First, Japanese people tend to .... For instance, ...
- As you can see, changing the rule would ...
- No matter how / when / who ...
- To sum up, ...

Decision Making ２人の経営者の話をもとに、会長は最終的な決断を下しましょう。経営者Ａと経営者Ｂの発言内容を簡単に振り返りながら、決断の理由を明確に示しましょう。

	President's Decision
結論	I decided (to / not to) accept people with tattoos because A/B gave me a good reason.
まとめ・理由	・A/B said that _____ . ・The opinion was very persuasive to me. ・A/B's idea of ( ) is good, but _____ .

Review Your Role Play Role Play を振り返って、自分がどのように話したかをチェックしましょう。

Q1 結論を述べたり、発言や論点をまとめたりするときの表現を使いましたか。

☐ 何度か使った　　☐ 1回使った　　☐ 使わなかった

Q2 Cue Expressionsやそれと同等の機能を持つ表現を使いましたか。

☐ 何度か使った　　☐ 1回使った　　☐ 使わなかった

Q3 メッセージを伝えるときに、〈no matter ＋ 疑問詞〉を使ってみましたか。

☐ 何度か使った　　☐ 1回使った　　☐ 使わなかった

Q4 自分の主張に対して、理由を明確に述べることができましたか。

☐ 複数の理由を述べた　　☐ 1つの理由を述べた　　☐ 理由を述べられなかった

Write Your Opinion

この章で学んだ語句を３つ以上使って、次のテーマについて100語以上のパラグラフを書きましょう。 ⇨解答欄は p. 144

Theme If you were the president of the association, would you accept people with tattoos?

Further Activities

この章で学んだ内容に関連する情報を追加で調べ、クラスメイトとシェアしましょう。

Example さまざまな国のタトゥーや入れ墨の現状や歴史などについて、調べてみましょう。

Appendix

Writing Worksheets

for *Write Your Opinion*

Unit 1で学んだ語句を3つ以上使って、100語以上のパラグラフを書きましょう。

Theme If you were the club leader, would you choose camping or staying at a hotel?

主題文	If I were the club leader, I would choose .... I have two reasons.
根拠1	First, ...
根拠1の 例・説明	(For example,) ....
根拠2	Second, ...
根拠2の 例・説明	(For example,) ....
まとめ	In conclusion, ...

Review Your Writing 書いた英文を読み直して次の点を確認しましょう。確認した項目の□にチェックを入れましょう。

1. **内 容**： □ 自分の意見を明示した　□ 学んだ事実・根拠を一部盛り込んだ
　　　　　　□ 独自の例を盛り込んだ　□ 学習した語句を3つ以上使った

2. **構 成**： □ 論理的パラグラフ（主題文＋支持文＋まとめ文）で書いている
　　　　　　□ 接続表現を使っている

3. **正確さ**： □ 文（S+V）で書けている　□ 時制　□ 単数・複数　□ 代名詞
　　　　　　□ カンマ・ピリオド　□ 品詞の用法

Write Your Opinion ──────────── Unit 2: Which is better for your health, tea or coffee?

Unit 2で学んだ語句を3つ以上使って、100語以上のパラグラフを書きましょう。

🖊️ **Theme** If you were the owner of the supermarket, would you promote tea or coffee?

主題文	If I were the owner, I would promote .... I have two reasons.
根拠1	First, ...
根拠1の 例・説明	(For example,) ....
根拠2	Second, ...
根拠2の 例・説明	(For example,) ....
まとめ	In conclusion, ...

Review Your Writing 書いた英文を読み直して次の点を確認しましょう。確認した項目の□にチェックを入れましょう。

1. **内 容**： □ 自分の意見を明示した　□ 学んだ事実・根拠を一部盛り込んだ
　　　　　　 □ 独自の例を盛り込んだ　□ 学習した語句を3つ以上使った

2. **構 成**： □ 論理的パラグラフ（主題文＋支持文＋まとめ文）で書いている
　　　　　　 □ 接続表現を使っている

3. **正確さ**： □ 文（S+V）で書けている　□ 時制　□ 単数・複数　□ 代名詞
　　　　　　 □ カンマ・ピリオド　□ 品詞の用法

Write Your Opinion

Unit 3: Which class style is more effective, face-to-face or online?

Unit 3で学んだ語句を3つ以上使って、100語以上のパラグラフを書きましょう。

Theme If you were Student A, would you take the course on campus or online?

主題文	If I were Student A, I would take the course .... I have two reasons.
根拠1	First, ...
根拠1の 例・説明	(For example,) ....
根拠2	Second, ...
根拠2の 例・説明	(For example,) ....
まとめ	In conclusion, ...

Review Your Writing 書いた英文を読み直して次の点を確認しましょう。確認した項目の□にチェックを入れましょう。

1. 内 容: □ 自分の意見を明示した　□ 学んだ事実・根拠を一部盛り込んだ
　　　　　□ 独自の例を盛り込んだ　□ 学習した語句を3つ以上使った

2. 構 成: □ 論理的パラグラフ（主題文＋支持文＋まとめ文）で書いている
　　　　　□ 接続表現を使っている

3. 正確さ: □ 文（S+V）で書けている　□ 時制　□ 単数・複数　□ 代名詞
　　　　　□ カンマ・ピリオド　□ 品詞の用法

Write Your Opinion ——————————— Unit 4: Which do you prefer, buying clothes or renting them?

Unit 4で学んだ語句を3つ以上使って、100語以上のパラグラフを書きましょう。

✏️ *Theme*　If you were Student A, would you buy your clothes or subscribe to a rental service?

主題文	If I were Student A, I would .... I have two reasons.
根拠1	First, ...
根拠1の 例・説明	(For example,) ....
根拠2	Second, ...
根拠2の 例・説明	(For example,) ....
まとめ	In conclusion, ...

Review Your Writing　書いた英文を読み直して次の点を確認しましょう。確認した項目の□にチェックを入れましょう。

1. **内 容：** □ 自分の意見を明示した　□ 学んだ事実・根拠を一部盛り込んだ
　　　　　　 □ 独自の例を盛り込んだ　□ 学習した語句を3つ以上使った

2. **構 成：** □ 論理的パラグラフ（主題文＋支持文＋まとめ文）で書いている
　　　　　　 □ 接続表現を使っている

3. **正確さ：** □ 文（S+V）で書けている　□ 時制　□ 単数・複数　□ 代名詞
　　　　　　 □ カンマ・ピリオド　□ 品詞の用法

Write Your Opinion

Unit 5で学んだ語句を3つ以上使って、100語以上のパラグラフを書きましょう。

Theme If you were the leader of the host city, would you include eSports in the Olympics?

主題文	If I were the leader of the host city, I would .... eSports in the Olympics. I have two reasons.
根拠1	First, ...
根拠1の例・説明	(For example,) ....
根拠2	Second, ...
根拠2の例・説明	(For example,) ....
まとめ	In conclusion, ...

Review Your Writing 書いた英文を読み直して次の点を確認しましょう。確認した項目の□にチェックを入れましょう。

1. 内 容： □ 自分の意見を明示した　□ 学んだ事実・根拠を一部盛り込んだ
□ 独自の例を盛り込んだ　□ 学習した語句を3つ以上使った

2. 構 成： □ 論理的パラグラフ（主題文＋支持文＋まとめ文）で書いている
□ 接続表現を使っている

3. 正確さ： □ 文(S+V)で書けている　□ 時制　□ 単数・複数　□ 代名詞
□ カンマ・ピリオド　□ 品詞の用法

Write Your Opinion ───────────── Unit 6: Should food companies abandon best-before dates?

Unit 6で学んだ語句を3つ以上使って、100語以上のパラグラフを書きましょう。

Theme If you were the CEO, would you abandon best-before dates?

主題文	If I were the CEO, I would .... best-before dates. I have two reasons.
根拠1	First, ...
根拠1の 例・説明	(For example,) ....
根拠2	Second, ...
根拠2の 例・説明	(For example,) ....
まとめ	In conclusion, ...

Review Your Writing 書いた英文を読み直して次の点を確認しましょう。確認した項目の□にチェッククを入れましょう。

1. 内 容： □ 自分の意見を明示した　□ 学んだ事実・根拠を一部盛り込んだ
　　　　　□ 独自の例を盛り込んだ　□ 学習した語句を3つ以上使った

2. 構 成： □ 論理的パラグラフ（主題文＋支持文＋まとめ文）で書いている
　　　　　□ 接続表現を使っている

3. 正確さ： □ 文（S+V）で書けている　□ 時制　□ 単数・複数　□ 代名詞
　　　　　□ カンマ・ピリオド　□ 品詞の用法

Write Your Opinion ———— Unit 7: Where do you like to watch movies, at a theater or at home?

Unit 7で学んだ語句を3つ以上使って、100語以上のパラグラフを書きましょう。

✍️
Theme If you were Student A, would you watch a movie with your friends at a theater or at home?

主題文	If I were Student A, I would watch a movie with my friends at .... I have two reasons.
根拠1	First, ...
根拠1の例・説明	(For example,) ....
根拠2	Second, ...
根拠2の例・説明	(For example,) ....
まとめ	In conclusion, ...

Review Your Writing 書いた英文を読み直して次の点を確認しましょう。確認した項目の□にチェックを入れましょう。

1. 内 容: □ 自分の意見を明示した　□ 学んだ事実・根拠を一部盛り込んだ
　　　　　　□ 独自の例を盛り込んだ　□ 学習した語句を3つ以上使った

2. 構 成: □ 論理的パラグラフ（主題文＋支持文＋まとめ文）で書いている
　　　　　　□ 接続表現を使っている

3. 正確さ: □ 文（S+V）で書けている　□ 時制　□ 単数・複数　□ 代名詞
　　　　　　□ カンマ・ピリオド　□ 品詞の用法

Write Your Opinion ———————————————— Unit 8: Should homeowners install solar panels?

Unit 8で学んだ語句を3つ以上使って、100語以上のパラグラフを書きましょう。

✍️ *Theme*　If you were the mayor, would you require new homeowners to install solar panels?

主題文	If I were the mayor, I would .... new homeowners to install solar panels. I have two reasons.
根拠1	First, ...
根拠1の 例・説明	(For example,) ....
根拠2	Second, ...
根拠2の 例・説明	(For example,) ....
まとめ	In conclusion, ...

(Review Your Writing)　書いた英文を読み直して次の点を確認しましょう。確認した項目の□にチェッククを入れましょう。

1. 内　容：　□ 自分の意見を明示した　□ 学んだ事実・根拠を一部盛り込んだ
　　　　　　□ 独自の例を盛り込んだ　□ 学習した語句を3つ以上使った

2. 構　成：　□ 論理的パラグラフ（主題文＋支持文＋まとめ文）で書いている
　　　　　　□ 接続表現を使っている

3. 正確さ：　□ 文（S+V）で書けている　□ 時制　□ 単数・複数　□ 代名詞
　　　　　　□ カンマ・ピリオド　□ 品詞の用法

Write Your Opinion

Unit 9で学んだ語句を3つ以上使って、100語以上のパラグラフを書きましょう。

Theme If you were the Minister of the Environment, would you ban the sale of pets?

主題文	If I were the minister, I would .... the sale of pets. I have two reasons.
根拠1	First, ...
根拠1の例・説明	(For example,) ....
根拠2	Second, ...
根拠2の例・説明	(For example,) ....
まとめ	In conclusion, ...

Review Your Writing 書いた英文を読み直して次の点を確認しましょう。確認した項目の□にチェッククを入れましょう。

1. 内 容： □ 自分の意見を明示した　□ 学んだ事実・根拠を一部盛り込んだ
　　　　　　 □ 独自の例を盛り込んだ　□ 学習した語句を3つ以上使った

2. 構 成： □ 論理的パラグラフ（主題文＋支持文＋まとめ文）で書いている
　　　　　　 □ 接続表現を使っている

3. 正確さ： □ 文（S＋V）で書けている　□ 時制　□ 単数・複数　□ 代名詞
　　　　　　 □ カンマ・ピリオド　□ 品詞の用法

Write Your Opinion

Unit 10: Should Japan introduce a four-day workweek?

Unit 10で学んだ語句を3つ以上使って、100語以上のパラグラフを書きましょう。

Theme　If you were the CEO, would you introduce a four-day workweek?

主題文	If I were the CEO, I would .... a four-day workweek. I have two reasons.
根拠1	First, ...
根拠1の 例・説明	(For example,) ....
根拠2	Second, ...
根拠2の 例・説明	(For example,) ....
まとめ	In conclusion, ...

Review Your Writing　書いた英文を読み直して次の点を確認しましょう。確認した項目の□にチェックを入れましょう。

1. 内　容：　□ 自分の意見を明示した　□ 学んだ事実・根拠を一部盛り込んだ
　　　　　　　□ 独自の例を盛り込んだ　□ 学習した語句を3つ以上使った

2. 構　成：　□ 論理的パラグラフ（主題文＋支持文＋まとめ文）で書いている
　　　　　　　□ 接続表現を使っている

3. 正確さ：　□ 文（S＋V）で書けている　□ 時制　□ 単数・複数　□ 代名詞
　　　　　　　□ カンマ・ピリオド　□ 品詞の用法

Write Your Opinion ——————————— Unit 11: Should children's video game time be limited by law?

Unit 11で学んだ語句を３つ以上使って、100語以上のパラグラフを書きましょう。

Theme ✏️ If you were the mayor, would you make an ordinance that limits children's video game time?

主題文	If I were the mayor, I would .... an ordinance that limits children's video game time. I have two reasons.
根拠１	First, ...
根拠１の 例・説明	(For example,) ....
根拠２	Second, ...
根拠２の 例・説明	(For example,) ....
まとめ	In conclusion, ...

Review Your Writing 書いた英文を読み直して次の点を確認しましょう。確認した項目の□にチェッククを入れましょう。

1. 内　容： □ 自分の意見を明示した　□ 学んだ事実・根拠を一部盛り込んだ
　　　　　　□ 独自の例を盛り込んだ　□ 学習した語句を３つ以上使った

2. 構　成： □ 論理的パラグラフ（主題文＋支持文＋まとめ文）で書いている
　　　　　　□ 接続表現を使っている

3. 正確さ： □ 文（S＋V）で書けている　□ 時制　□ 単数・複数　□ 代名詞
　　　　　　□ カンマ・ピリオド　□ 品詞の用法

Write Your Opinion ── Unit 12: Should cashless payment be promoted further in Japan?

Unit 12で学んだ語句を3つ以上使って、100語以上のパラグラフを書きましょう。

✍️ *Theme* If you were the mayor, would you promote cashless payment further in your city?

主題文	If I were the mayor, I would _____ cashless payment further in the city. I have two reasons.
根拠1	First, _____ .
根拠1の例・説明	(For example,) _____ .
根拠2	Second, _____ .
根拠2の例・説明	(For example,) _____ .
まとめ	In conclusion, _____ .

Review Your Writing 書いた英文を読み直して次の点を確認しましょう。確認した項目の□にチェックを入れましょう。

1. 内 容: □ 自分の意見を明示した　□ 学んだ事実・根拠を一部盛り込んだ
　　　　　　□ 独自の例を盛り込んだ　□ 学習した語句を3つ以上使った

2. 構 成: □ 論理的パラグラフ(主題文+支持文+まとめ文)で書いている
　　　　　　□ 接続表現を使っている

3. 正確さ: □ 文(S+V)で書けている　□ 時制　□ 単数・複数　□ 代名詞
　　　　　　□ カンマ・ピリオド　□ 品詞の用法

Write Your Opinion —————— Unit 13: Should social media companies censor their platforms?

Unit 13で学んだ語句を3つ以上使って、100語以上のパラグラフを書きましょう。

Theme If you were the CEO, would you censor your social media platform?

主題文	If I were the CEO, I would .... our social media platform. I have two reasons.
根拠1	First, ...
根拠1の 例・説明	(For example,) ....
根拠2	Second, ...
根拠2の 例・説明	(For example,) ....
まとめ	In conclusion, ...

Review Your Writing 書いた英文を読み直して次の点を確認しましょう。確認した項目の□にチェックを入れましょう。

1. 内　容 : □ 自分の意見を明示した　□ 学んだ事実・根拠を一部盛り込んだ
　　　　　　 □ 独自の例を盛り込んだ　□ 学習した語句を3つ以上使った

2. 構　成 : □ 論理的パラグラフ（主題文＋支持文＋まとめ文）で書いている
　　　　　　 □ 接続表現を使っている

3. 正確さ : □ 文(S+V)で書けている　□ 時制　□ 単数・複数　□ 代名詞
　　　　　　 □ カンマ・ピリオド　□ 品詞の用法

Write Your Opinion ——————— Unit 14: Should Japan invest more in space development?

Unit 14で学んだ語句を3つ以上使って、100語以上のパラグラフを書きましょう。

✍️ **Theme** If you were the Minister of MEXT, would you invest more in space development?

主題文	If I were the minister, I would .... more in space development. I have two reasons.
根拠1	First, ...
根拠1の 例・説明	(For example,) ....
根拠2	Second, ...
根拠2の 例・説明	(For example,) ....
まとめ	In conclusion, ...

Review Your Writing 書いた英文を読み直して次の点を確認しましょう。確認した項目の□にチェッククを入れましょう。

1. 内 容: □ 自分の意見を明示した　□ 学んだ事実・根拠を一部盛り込んだ
　　　　　　□ 独自の例を盛り込んだ　□ 学習した語句を3つ以上使った

2. 構 成: □ 論理的パラグラフ（主題文＋支持文＋まとめ文）で書いている
　　　　　　□ 接続表現を使っている

3. 正確さ: □ 文（S+V）で書けている　□ 時制　□ 単数・複数　□ 代名詞
　　　　　　□ カンマ・ピリオド　□ 品詞の用法

Write Your Opinion —— Unit 15: Should public baths and hot springs accept people with tattoos?

Unit 15で学んだ語句を3つ以上使って、100語以上のパラグラフを書きましょう。

✍ **Theme** If you were the president of the association, would you accept people with tattoos?

主題文	If I were the president, I would .... people with tattoos. I have two reasons.
根拠1	First, ...
根拠1の 例・説明	(For example,) ....
根拠2	Second, ...
根拠2の 例・説明	(For example,) ....
まとめ	In conclusion, ...

Review Your Writing 書いた英文を読み直して次の点を確認しましょう。確認した項目の□にチェックを入れましょう。

1. **内 容**： □ 自分の意見を明示した □ 学んだ事実・根拠を一部盛り込んだ
   □ 独自の例を盛り込んだ □ 学習した語句を3つ以上使った

2. **構 成**： □ 論理的パラグラフ（主題文＋支持文+まとめ文）で書いている
   □ 接続表現を使っている

3. **正確さ**： □ 文（S+V）で書けている □ 時制 □ 単数・複数 □ 代名詞
   □ カンマ・ピリオド □ 品詞の用法

本書にはCD（別売）があります

Voice Your Opinion
ディスカッションで伸ばす 発信型英語演習

2023年1月20日　初版第1刷発行
2024年2月20日　初版第3刷発行

著　者　　飯　野　　厚
　　　　　中　村　さ　よ
　　　　　Brian Wistner
　　　　　和　田　俊　彦
　　　　　籔　田　由己子

発行者　　福　岡　正　人
発行所　　株式会社　金　星　堂

（〒101-0051）　東京都千代田区神田神保町 3-21
　　　　Tel　（03）3263-3828（営業部）
　　　　　　　（03）3263-3997（編集部）
　　　　Fax　（03）3263-0716
　　　　https://www.kinsei-do.co.jp

編集担当　四條雪菜・戸田浩平　　　　　　　　Printed in Japan
印刷所・製本所／三美印刷株式会社

ISBN978-4-7647-4179-9　C1082